A
TOOLKIT
FOR
MODERN
LIFE

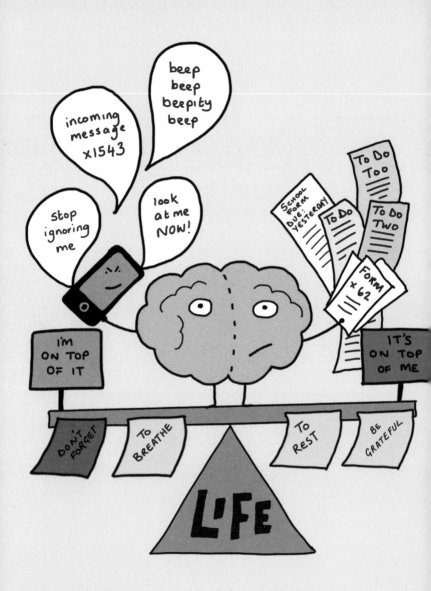

A
TOOLKIT
FOR
MODERN
LIFE

53 WAYS TO LOOK AFTER YOUR MIND

Dr Emma Hepburn
@thepsychologymum

greenfinch

Contents

WHAT MENTAL HEALTH IS OFTEN DEFINED AS:

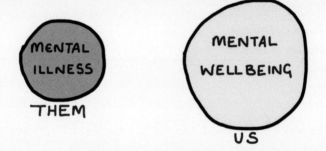

WHAT MENTAL HEALTH ACTUALLY IS:

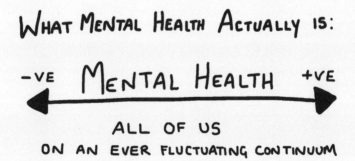

Introduction: Looking After Your Mind

Modern life is busy. We are all trying to find the seemingly impossible balance of work and home – keeping other people happy, searching for our own happiness, looking after our finances, looking after children, searching for body positivity, juggling to-do lists, trying to slow down. It all requires scheduling, messaging, updating, bullet-listing – all with the background noise of technology that promises time-saving while often creating more demand, alerting you to WhatsApp messages, Facebook and Instagram updates. It's a bleeping, buzzing world of notifications, where everybody looks like they've got it more together than you.

In reality, we are all juggling life, with balls dropping and curveballs being thrown when we least expect it. None of us ever gets it right all the time, and we constantly fluctuate between feeling on top of life and feeling like life is on top of us. I'm not promising you will find the magical balance in this book, but I am hoping you will find ways to look after one of the most important aspects in your life: your mind.

Your mind is at the centre of your story – watching, planning, responding, remembering, developing, interacting and creating as you go along. Looking after your mind might not be the whole story, but it is crucial to *your* story and you need to nurture it. This book will help you to develop a personal toolkit to look after your mind, to navigate your world, your story and whatever modern life throws at you.

Debunking myths

The mind is synonymous with mental health, so looking after your mind is also about looking after your mental health. To do this, we need to bust some of the myths that surround mental health. Firstly, we simply need to recognize that we all have mental health that needs looking after.

We need to shift away from the concept that mental health is something that other people have, and that we only need to think about reactively when it goes wrong. Mental health is something that we all have and need to look after proactively. We need to understand that, just like physical health, mental health is changeable and can vary throughout life. It sometimes needs extra care, and given the right (or wrong) mix of situations and person, anyone's mental health can suffer. Rather than seeing this as a flaw, we need to understand the contributing factors and know how we can help or seek help. We need to recognize that mental health is not all in the brain – it is fundamentally linked to our bodies, as well as the environment in which we live. It's about learning the signs that our mental health is deteriorating so we can take action to help as best we can.

The mental health jam jar

We all have a mental health jam jar that gets filled with our vulnerabilities (strawberries) and stressors (raspberries). Everybody's vulnerabilities will be at different levels and their stressors will change throughout life. This analogy has been used to describe genetic vulnerabilities by professor and genetic counsellor Jehannine Austin, but as a psychologist I like to consider a range of vulnerabilities including biological, social, cognitive, environmental and life experiences. We all have a certain limit, and if these stressors exceed our jam-jar level, it triggers mental health difficulties. We can increase the space in our jar by learning and using coping strategies, such as social support, good sleep and exercise.

This concept shows that everyone has mental health to consider and limits to that mental health. Secondly, it demonstrates that anyone's mental health can suffer, depending on what's going on in life. Thirdly, it considers people's background and experience, which can help explain why some people are more vulnerable than others to mental health difficulties. What I like most about this concept is that it is a hopeful model, as it shows that we have the ability to increase our resilience through managing stressors (if possible) and using coping strategies. This book focuses on looking after your mind, by helping increase your jar's space and by managing the raspberries.

your Mental Health Jam Jar

We all have a Mental Health Jam Jar

It is filled with our
🍇 = vulnerabilities
🍓 = stressors

Full = distress/poor mental health

Supportive friends

CHEERLEADER CHUTNEY

Exercise

Our jar can become bigger by using helpful coping strategies

But what is a mind?

Well, this question is debated and not always clear, so I'll explain how I understand it. The mind is where you experience your internal and external world and who you are. It's where you hear your thoughts and where you perceive, feel, understand, remember and view yourself, the world and your place in it. It's also how you interact with the world. It's constructed by your brain, but it's not just your brain.

I see the mind as a three-piece band consisting of your brain, body and environment. It's a finely tuned band that takes you through life, playing different harmonies, each being required for the full song to sound correct. So to speak about your brain without your body or environment would be to leave out two-thirds of the band: it's Destiny without her Child. (Yes, Beyoncé – or your brain – is fantastic, but the songs are incomplete without the other members.)

Let's break this down further, to show how these elements together form your mind. Your brain controls and regulates your physical functions, and is responsible for cognition that allows you to navigate the world: thoughts, memories, planning, organizing, attention, decision-making. It is also where you understand emotions, which you require for a host of functions. Inside your brain are billions of neurons with links to other neurons, communicating with each other through electrical impulses along super-highways at top speed. These neurons enable your brain to be an expert communicator that understands and shapes your world and how you respond to it. But your brain doesn't communicate only with itself; it communicates with your body and also takes feedback from your body. And on this two-way highway, your body affects your brain and mind, and vice versa. For example, how we think and feel affects our experience of pain: our beliefs about medicine affect how effective they are; chronic stress is linked to lowered immune systems and a range of illnesses; physical exercise can be effective in treating mental health.

Even more remarkably, your body and brain are also closely interlinked with your environment. The world shapes your brain, and therefore mind, and your brain shapes how you see your environment. You perceive it based on what you know about it so far, your experiences. As we are social beings, the people in your environment also influence your brain. Your caregiver as you grow up influences how you respond to the environment and helps shape your beliefs and behaviours. We constantly influence each other's brains through life – our brains react to what we think other people are experiencing. We imagine and, therefore, feel their pain. Our environment is so linked to how our brain and body function that we cannot think about the mind without taking into account the environment in which that mind exists.

So, when we consider how to look after your mind in this book, we'll look at the three parts of brain, body and environment. Each part contributes to your mind and, therefore, together they are the basis for looking after it. In the same way, mental health is not considered solely in the brain (or in the mind) – it is considered as a whole body construct.

So, what do we mean by a healthy mind?

Contrary to popular belief, a healthy mind is not one that feels happy all the time and doesn't feel sadness or other (what we might perceive as) negative emotions. As we will find out, these emotions are necessary in life. To me, a healthy mind is one that can help you look after yourself and treat yourself respectfully, with kindness and compassion. It allows you to understand your emotions and respond to them in a way that is helpful to you, so that you can manage stressors that life throws at you and make the most of your life. What a healthy mind means to you might be different. It's worth thinking about your own meaning, so you can recognize when your mind deviates from this, and when you may need to take extra steps to look after it.

How to use the toolkit

We all need a bag of mental health tools to get us through life. While there are similarities in how we experience the world, no two people are the same and we will all have our own set of tools that are helpful to us. The tools we need will also change depending on the circumstances at any particular time.

This book will guide you through a range of mental health tools, using evidence-based models. These techniques have been selected based on my experiences of working with a wide range of people. They are the tools that people have told me they find most helpful – those they come back to again and again, to enable them to live their lives more effectively.

As you read through the book, identify and select the mental health tools that are most helpful to you. Your toolkit can be added to at any time: you may find that some tools are getting rusty and need an update, or you may require a completely new one when life takes you somewhere different. It is helpful to keep your notes in the same place (either by scribbling over the pages of this book, or keeping a separate notebook), so that whenever you face challenges you can refer back to the exercises you have done that have been useful to you.

This book doesn't need to be read in a linear way; you can select the topics that you need right now. Once you have filled your toolkit, it will be a resource you can turn to again and again to tackle the many things that modern life can throw at you.

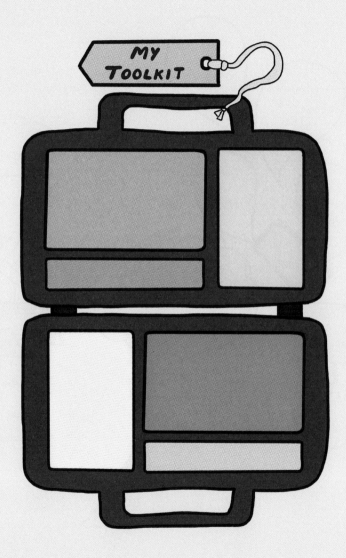

Chapter 1
Building the Foundations of Mental Wellbeing

Looking after your mind and mental health proactively –
what does that really mean? And aren't the solutions to
achieving positive mental health expensive and complex?
Well, yes, mental health can be complex, and it's not always
easy to work out what's going on and what to do about it.
But I want to move away from the idea that looking after
your mental health is mysterious and unobtainable, or that
there's a magical elixir that dissolves all your problems,
allowing you to ride off into a happy rainbow-filled future,
never to feel sad again. Searching for the 'potion', or the
ultimate answer, can make us feel impotent, as taking care
of our mental health seems so out of our control. We also
have a tendency to dismiss simple things that have the
greatest impact. In reality, while treatments for mental ill
health need to be individual to a person's unique needs,
what actually helps your mind and your health on a day-to-
day basis – both mental and physical – are those daily
habits that are tangible and obtainable. This chapter guides
you through taking small steps to help you manage
stressors and find achievable ways to look after your mind.

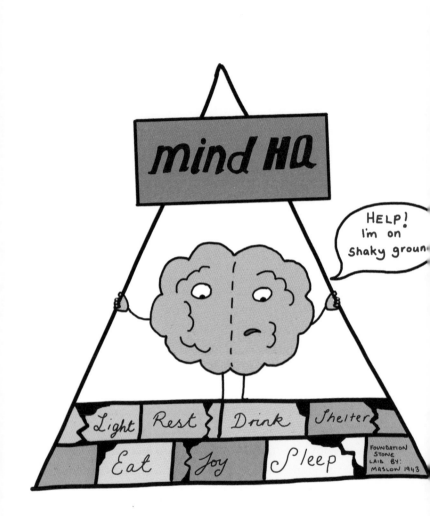

Don't forget the basics

How we feel is intrinsically linked to our bodies. If you are tired, thirsty, ill or hungry, you're likely to feel bad to some extent. And when you feel rubbish, you are more likely to have unpleasant thoughts, and less likely to do things that make you feel good. On a more complex level, poor sleep, lack of exercise and illness all impact on how your body and brain work. Feeling bad because of the basics can then cascade into other patterns of thoughts and behaviours, which can become a vicious cycle.

Your brain is constantly interpreting how you feel, in relation to your environment and based on your past experiences, so that you can respond. When your body feels unpleasant it can be a sign that something is out of kilter. Many things can affect your body and make you feel a bit 'wrong': hunger, thirst, illness, needing the toilet, tiredness, pain. Some of these, like hunger or thirst, are easier to regulate than others and can be remedied quickly. But the brain is not a perfect system, and sometimes in its quest for meaning it misinterprets simple body signals. How often have you been confused about why you are feeling so bad and analysed it endlessly with no outcome? In the middle of analysing, you mindlessly eat a sandwich, then all of a sudden things seem much better. The rush of energy and blood sugar from that sandwich has regulated your body and improved your mood. You felt rubbish because you were hungry, but the analytical brain sometimes overlooks the simple answer in the search for a higher meaning.

It's important to take care of the physical body to avoid negative consequences for how you feel. But the basics are not just about managing unpleasant feelings; it is just as important to think about creating pleasant feelings. While getting essentials right, like sleep and diet, is more likely to make us feel good, enjoyment, rest and relaxation are also basic needs which we can plan for.

The term 'self-care' tends to get overused these days, in ad campaigns for just about any product under the sun, but its importance should not be underplayed. Looking after yourself provides the building blocks that create strong foundations that both strengthen our mental health and provide greater long-term resilience in the face of life's inevitable rocky road. I've chosen to focus on sleep, diet, enjoyment and relaxation in the exercises here, but other basics could include looking after your physical health (e.g. medical check-ups), your living environment, your financial situation and getting natural light. Identify if there are any gaps in your foundations and target these when you can.

Filling the gaps in your foundations: sleep

Poor sleep can not only make you feel rubbish, it can also affect your cognition and your health. With less sleep, you may be less able to engage in tasks, maintain your focus or remember information. Sleep is also thought to have a specific function in encoding memories, so it's no surprise you feel more absent-minded and forgetful after a poor night's rest. Recent research indicates sleep may be the nightshift when the brain's caretakers, the glial cells, are hardest at work, mopping up all the debris. So it's important to get enough good quality sleep.

The ironic thing is the more you try to sleep, the harder it can be. The gap between going to bed and actual sleep provides a space that your mind can fill with all sorts of worries. And when we are worried or experiencing higher stress, our sleep patterns can change and we may find we wake more frequently or have more nightmares. If you have recurring sleep problems, speak to your doctor, as a referral to a sleep clinic may be necessary.

Tick off any of the sleep barriers listed on the following pages that resonate with you and try to tackle these problems with the solutions provided.

Sleep barrier: general worry

1. Write down your worries before bedtime so that you can deal with these in the morning. Then if worry pops into your head, remind yourself that you will be dealing with it tomorrow.

2. Focus on slow breathing, listening to and feeling your breath (a breathing or relaxation app such as Headspace or Calm can help).

3. Distract yourself with relaxing audio books or podcasts.

Sleep barrier: trouble switching off a busy brain

1. Avoid activities that energize you or get you thinking too much before bed.

2. Practise sleep rituals that are the same every night, such as having a warm shower, a hot drink or reading a few pages of a book. This can help settle you and create associations with sleep.

3. Dim the lights before bedtime.

4. Don't eat too late at night and avoid caffeine after late afternoon.

5. Avoid naps during the day.

Sleep barrier: worry about getting to sleep or trying too hard to get to sleep

1. Remind yourself that you will be able to cope, even with just a few hours of sleep.

2. Try any of the relaxation or distraction techniques mentioned in the solutions to the previous sleep barriers.

3. Try not to sleep – this might seem strange but there's evidence that it works for some people.

4. Get out of bed and do something relaxing, then return to bed when sleepy.

Sleep barrier: not getting enough sleep

1. Reset the value and meaning of sleep – it is not for the weak, it improves everything.

2. Prioritize sleep and plan when to go to bed and wake up. Going to bed and waking up at consistent times has been shown to improve sleep.

3. Keep your bed for sleeping, not working or checking your phone.

4. Keep electronic devices out of the bedroom so that you don't check them during the night. Blue light wakes your brain up and disrupts melatonin release.

Filling the gaps in your foundations: diet

Your body and brain need water and food to function effectively, at a cell level and beyond. Therefore, not eating or drinking enough water can make people feel grumpy, along with a whole range of other unpleasant feelings. Luckily, eating a varied diet, with lots of fruit and vegetables, can impact positively on both your general health and brain health.

Food can also be a great source of pleasure, allowing us to pause, rest and create positive emotions. However, due to the societal messages we encounter about food and weight, our relationship with food can be incredibly complex. Our moods can make us crave particular foods and then we shame ourselves for eating them. Our busy lives can mean we eat mindlessly. We restrict our diet, which may make us feel good in the short term but has a negative effect long term.

And what about drinks? We can forget to drink water, leading to dehydration, which can make us feel tired. We over-fuel our exhaustion with that readily available drug caffeine, which engages that flight/fight system. (One of the most effective treatments I once used for anxiety was weaning someone off a famous soft drink, which at the time had high levels of caffeine.) We use alcohol to manage how we feel, but yet, all too often the alcohol has a negative effect on brain functioning – lucky you, if you've never felt that hangover dread.

There are general tweaks you can make to your diet that can impact positively on your mind. However, if you find your relationship with food is making it difficult for you to eat a varied diet, eat regularly or even enjoy food, you should speak to your GP or healthcare professional.

Use the following checklist to identify your eating and drinking habits. Think about any ways that food and drink are impacting negatively on how you feel, and tweaks that you can make for a positive impact.

☐ *Do I eat regularly?*

☐ *Do I restrict my diet?*

☐ *Do I eat a varied diet, including fruit and vegetables?*

☐ *Do I drink enough fluids regularly?*

☐ *Do I consume too much caffeine?*

☐ *Do I consume too much alcohol?*

☐ *Do I sit down to eat a meal?*

☐ *Do I savour my meal and eat slowly?*

Planning joy and relaxation

It is easy to just react to what life throws at you and overlook doing things that bring you joy and relaxation. You may feel you don't have time for them, or don't value them, or yourself, enough. I often joke in my work that 'the psychologist has prescribed a holiday' when people feel guilty about doing something nice for themselves. The benefits of giving yourself a treat are two-fold: the positive impact of doing the thing itself; and the positive feelings you experience as you anticipate, think and plan for something you are looking forward to. Although we all love a holiday, this isn't always possible. However, planning joy doesn't have to be about big things – in fact, the more small things interspersed throughout the week, the better. Scheduling them in your diary, rather than slotting them into gaps, means you are more likely to do them.

The barriers to this 'joy schedule' are guilt, time, the sense that it's not important and lack of planning, but experiencing enjoyable activities are critical in your life as they will help you manage stress effectively, help you relax and engage your body's healing and recovery systems. Tiny little pockets of enjoyment and relaxation are as good as big ones and can be planned even during difficult times. These small moments of joy can guide you back to feeling better or feeling more like yourself. Michelle Obama speaks about planning joy, not just planning work, and teaching ourselves to take time to plan those things we enjoy to keep ourselves healthy. And if Michelle can do it, then so can we.

Use the following questions to think about how you can introduce more joy and relaxation to your everyday life.

What small daily things can I do that bring me joy?

What small daily things can I do that help me relax?

How can I fit these into my life?

What are my barriers to planning joy and relaxation?

How can I make sure these don't fall off my to-do list?

5 Pillars of Mental Health

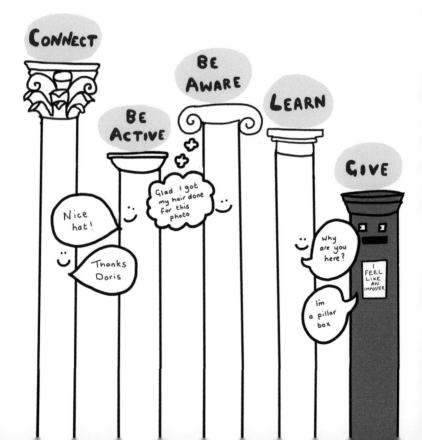

The 5 pillars of mental health

I'd like to introduce you to the five pillars. While they may not agree on everything, they are quite confident that each of them has something worthwhile to bring to your life. There is good evidence that these five things can positively influence your mental health and mind.

Pillar 1: Connect

Humans are social animals, and there is increasing evidence that isolation is detrimental to our health. Being with people who make us feel safe and secure, who we share experiences with and have fun with, can induce positive emotions, regulate our body and is a key component of a healthy mind. It gives us an opportunity to talk things through, validating and making sense of our thoughts, emotions and experiences. It can help us problem-solve difficult situations, as well as widening our thinking and enabling us to see other perspectives. We learn from other people, which is inherently good for the brain and mind.

There's evidence that having good relationships is the strongest factor in keeping us happy and healthy. In a world saturated with self-care soundbites, it can be easy to overlook the fact that *collective* care is more effective for our wellbeing. It's not always easy to achieve if you have had experiences in the past that make it difficult to trust people, or find yourself isolated for whatever reason. In addition, when we feel bad, we often want to hide away, and seeing other people can feel overwhelming. The key is to connect with people who make you feel good, whom you trust, and with whom you share interests and values. Even if it feels hard, it's worth making the effort to create and sustain connections, because of the profound benefits this can have for you and your mind.

Pillar 2: Be active

We all know that exercise is good for physical health; as the brain is a physical organ, it should come as no surprise that exercise is good for it too. Exercise gets blood pumping through your body, keeps your inner organs, veins and arteries working well (and there are a lot of them in your brain), gives you a sense of achievement, and releases some lovely chemicals – endorphins – that produce pleasant feelings and decrease your body's stress responses. Exercise has been shown to improve brain functioning, too, as well as cognitive processes including attention, concentration and learning new information.

Exercise is beneficial at any age but the thought of it can be daunting. However, if you shift the emphasis to merely being active, it can seem much more manageable. Simply moving about can shift emotions, help clear the mind and give a sense of achievement. Don't disregard activities because you don't see them as traditional exercise – 'moving' can be a run or a walk, but it can also be cleaning, yoga, gardening, kitchen discos and even singing. Small, enjoyable movement is more likely to be incorporated into your life on a longer-term basis.

Pillar 3: Be aware

Much of the thinking space in the brain is taken up by past experiences and imaginary futures. There's nothing wrong with this: the brain is performing some of its key functions such as memory-making, planning, problem-solving and anticipating. However, sometimes this takes up so much of your limited brain space that you don't notice what is going on in the here and now. From a psychologist's point of view, you need to be aware of your feelings and emotions in the present moment in order to be able to spot problems and take action.

Paying attention to the present moment can also regulate your stress response, engage soothing body systems and have long-term health benefits. This idea is intrinsic to yoga, mindfulness and meditation. You can use some of the same principles to increase awareness in your everyday life. This may be as simple as engaging your attention fully in your environment or what you are doing: go for a walk and notice the colour of leaves on the trees, or notice the qualities of your ingredients, such as the smells, texture or colour, when cooking. You can also take your awareness to your body to help you understand how you are feeling and your needs. When working, for example, stop every now and then to think about how your body feels. Does it need a break or feel like a quick walk? Observe your breathing for a few moments. Notice your thought patterns – particularly helpful when you are experiencing difficult emotions – to help decide which thoughts to engage with and which just to notice and release.

Any activity that absorbs you fully in the present is beneficial. Creative activities, whether it's painting, card-making or exercise, can focus your attention on the here and now. For me, it's badminton! All I focus on is getting that shuttlecock back over the net and beating my husband. For some people it's writing, acting or singing. And, of course, all these activities have bonus effects on your mind of achievement, enjoyment and social connection.

Pillar 4: Learn

Learning keeps your brain active, making it form new links, and can give you a sense of purpose, helping you to develop new ideas. Research shows this is both good for how you feel and your brain as an organ and has long-term physical health benefits (there's that mind/body link again…). The brain develops on a cellular level as understanding develops. I find that amazing, and think of learning as a workout for the brain.

However, we can associate learning with stress, or even feeling inadequate or a failure. I still get a stress response thinking back to my last exams. But learning doesn't have to be about sitting exams, memorizing times tables or repeating tenses in foreign languages – it is about anything new that the brain can discover. It can be reading about something new, learning new words, discovering new places, trying a new activity or taste-testing foods (now that's my type of learning). My preferred learning method recently has been listening to podcasts and radio shows – they get me thinking, and are extremely interesting and relaxing to listen to, so a triple brain whammy!

Pillar 5: Give

Humans are fundamentally social beings and, in general, brains are designed to mirror other people's emotions – we feel their pain, we sense their discomfort – so that we can empathize with them. If you think that someone feels anxious, this can make you anxious too. Any parent of a screaming toddler will know how hard it is not to mirror those feelings and instead respond calmly. While, at times, this empathy can make us feel unpleasant, we can use it to help us feel good by giving to others.

You may have heard of the 'helper's high', when we feel good because we have done something good for others. Research shows that helping others leads to positive effects for the person helping: we feel better, regulate stress and strengthen social connections. It also has direct physiological benefits, including lowered blood pressure, and appears to improve health, both physical and mental. In fact, giving to others appears to have greater beneficial effect than being on the receiving end.

'Well, that's okay,' you say, 'but I don't have lots of spare money to give.' Incorporating giving into your life doesn't need to cost money. Time and consideration are commodities you can give: taking time to listen to others, offering to help someone, sending a thank-you note, telling your friend how much they mean to you. If you want to take this further (and have the time), try volunteering, giving to a food bank, helping plant bulbs in a local park, taking part in a reading scheme at your local school, or offering some cooked meals to someone going through a tough time. There are so many ways to give, you just need to think creatively about what you can do and how you can fit this into your life.

Using the pillars in your life

Fill in the diagram with ideas of how you might bring the 5 pillars into your life. Be as creative as possible about how you can use these principles in your everyday life.

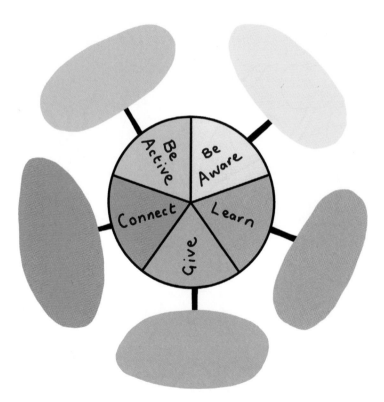

What do I value?

What is important to you? What's meaningful for you? I'm not asking what do you want to achieve from life. I'm asking what makes your life feel worthwhile? What makes you feel like you have used your limited time and energy in the best way possible? Yes, achievement might be part of it, but it's not the whole story. It's about engaging in activities and interacting with people in a way that is consistent with what you value. It's about prioritizing your values as central in your life.

Research suggests that living a life consistent with your values makes for a healthier mind. Connecting your values to your life, gives you purpose and meaning – essential human needs. It answers the question 'What is the point of life?', because the point is engaging with what fundamentally matters to you. If you've ever felt uncomfortable about doing something, or because of someone else's behaviour, it may have been because you were sensing that this was out of kilter with your values. Values help guide what you do and help you understand why you are feeling the way you do.

Your values are with you through good and bad times. I have guidelines and ethics that guide my professional practice, and, similarly, you can use personal guidelines and ethics to guide your life. Although you don't necessarily know what's coming your way, you can guide your responses in line with your values. Life is full of perpetual decisions, from small everyday ones you don't even have to think about, to huge life decisions that can have a major impact. While they won't necessarily make these decisions easy, values can be a helpful tool to make better decisions.

This is not something we tend to think about as we go about our everyday lives. I'd find it a bit weird if my friends asked, 'Hey, Emma, what are your values?' or 'Have you been meeting your values today?', when I just want to hear their opinion on the latest Netflix series. You may have thought about your values as part of a work appraisal, but there's no automatic appraisal to consider if your actions are consistent with your values in your life generally. So, let's do a life appraisal now.

What do I value?

Values are not how you feel or goals to reach, they are guides for action you will take through your life.

Think about all the things that are important to you and make a note of these on a piece of paper. Use the Values Tree (see page 36) for ideas and inspiration for common values that people identify. These questions may also help as a prompt:

What would I want people to remember about me?

If I was looking back on my life, what would I be most pleased about?

What characteristics do I most value in other people?

What am I doing when I am happiest?

What makes me feel most fulfilled and satisfied?

Once you have answered these questions, you may notice there are themes. Pull out four of the values or themes that are most important to you - these are your guiding values. I've made it sound nice and easy, but it can take time to work out your values, so I've put some resources in the Further Reading section (see pages 188-9) that may help you further.

Incorporating your values into your life

Now you can start thinking about areas in your life where you could be more consistent with your values. For example, if social connection is one of your values, what are you doing that incorporates this? Is there anything else you could do that would enable you to live up to this value? Could you message a friend you haven't seen in a while?

Write down the values you identified in Exercise 1 in the flags below. Write down ideas for how you can engage in these values, through actions in day-to-day life, in the body of each mountain. You may already be doing some, so write these in too.

Remember: ideas that are small and achievable are more likely to be successful. (My most recent idea was to only buy takeaway coffee when I remember my reusable cup, to fit in with my value of trying to look after the environment.)

Incorporating your Values into your Life

write your top values into the flags

write in here how you can live this value

Making decisions – the values signpost

The concept of a values signpost can help you to make decisions in line with your guiding principles. Visualize a signpost that has two arrows pointing in opposite directions: one points towards your values and the other points away from your values. This idea can be used in decision-making in two ways:

1. It can help you recognize *when* you are making choices and allow you to make an active decision, rather than just feeling like you are going along for the ride. For example, next time you pick up your phone, you can stop, consider the signpost and ask yourself whether this is moving you towards your values, e.g. connecting with friends or helping you relax, or is it moving you away, e.g. mindlessly scrolling through social media and making you feel inadequate?

2. It can help you make difficult decisions, by prompting you to think about which outcome best fits with your values. Use the signpost to consider in which direction your decision is taking you. Is it taking you towards your values or is it taking you further away? For example, will the new job enable you to engage in more activities consistent with your values or will it push you into activities at odds with your values?

Chapter 2
The Ups and Downs of Life

Some incredibly lucky people will go through life with very few stressful experiences or bad things happening. For most people, the reality is that life tends to throw curveballs – or sometimes even rocks – at them, creating a series of ups and downs, sideways steps and U-turns. We have to learn to navigate this pathway, and all the associated emotions on this sometimes bumpy road, as best we can. No matter how hard we try to control our life pathway, there can be unexpected turns, barriers on the road, dead ends and even major earthquakes. As a result, stress is an almost inevitable part of travelling along this road. While stress isn't always bad, it sometimes builds up to the point where you have more going on in your life than you have capacity for, both practically and emotionally, and your path takes you to 'overwhelm land' – a place where you can feel muddled, out of control and can't see where to go next. This chapter focuses on understanding and managing stress, using the capacity cup (see pages 44–51), and gives you tools to navigate stressful life events at those times when life does throw rocks at you.

The Capacity Cup

The capacity cup

Grab yourself a cup of tea, any cup will do. Tea not your thing? A beer mug or tall latte glass is just as good. In fact, any drinking vessel will do – oh, except an espresso cup or shot glass, they're far too small. Now sit back and enjoy the drink. No, hold on! Before you do, take a good look at that cup and think about it in a different way. Imagine the space inside the cup – it has limited capacity, and if it gets too full it will overflow. This cup represents your emotional capacity. It is your capacity cup.

We all have limited emotional capacity. Everything you do fills your cup. Mundane, small things might take up a tiny bit of capacity. Two small children running around requires more resources to manage, so takes up a larger amount of capacity. Do you have stressful life events coming up, a job interview or some medical tests? Capacity will be taken up planning and thinking about these. Even good things, such as planning a party or visiting friends, will use some capacity. How much capacity each thing takes up will be individual to you.

Things tend to sneak into our cup and it can reach the top before we even notice. Stressful things tend to use more capacity as we need more time, energy and brain space to think about them. At other times, your cup can be filled all in one go, when life throws major stressors at you.

Recognizing how full your capacity cup is at any one time can help manage stress. As you get nearer the top, you have less emotional capacity left. This means even a tiny thing can use all your remaining capacity and make your cup overflow. Have you ever felt devastated by a seemingly tiny thing such as a broken glass or no milk left at the shop, or overwhelmed by something you'd normally manage with ease? It's likely you didn't have the capacity to manage that thing.

This can be confusing. Why are you reacting so strongly to such a small thing? Why can't you do the thing that you would normally find so easy? When your cup has lots of capacity, these things cause minimal stress, as they only fill your cup slightly higher. However, when you are near the top, in the red zone, you are likely to react less rationally to situations, your emotions can be more intense and you can find it harder to plan and problem-solve. You just do not have the emotional capacity to step back, think about things clearly and deal with them.

What's filling your capacity cup?

Draw your cup on a piece of paper and then write down what's in your cup, i.e. what's using up your emotional capacity right now. Anything can use your capacity: worrying about other people, planning for future events, daily tasks such as work and looking after children, even being hungry or thirsty.

Each time you put something in the cup, draw a line to indicate the level your cup is at. This is subjective, as what might use minimal space for one person can use more for another. Also, the same thing can use different amounts of capacity at different times. For example, if you are working longer hours than usual, work will take up more capacity than it normally does.

You may have an underlying issue that takes up a lot of your capacity before you even start filling in what's going on in your everyday life. For example, if you are managing a medical condition and its related symptoms, this will fill up some of your cup. Pain and fatigue will also fill up your cup, and this may vary across days as the symptoms vary. As a result, you may have less baseline capacity on a regular basis. This is important to recognize and validate, as doing so can help you prioritize how to use your remaining capacity.

Now you've added everything in, how full is your cup? How much space do you have left? It can be surprising to see what is taking up most of your emotional capacity. Give yourself time to think about it, or talk things through with a friend. Being aware of your capacity cup, understanding what is filling it and how full up it is, can help you manage your capacity proactively, helping you to act before reaching the point of being overwhelmed.

Spotting the signs you are reaching red

When our capacity cup is near the brim, we tend to react less rationally, our thinking is more rigid, we can be irritable and our emotions tend to be bigger and more reactive. The trick to dealing with this is to notice the warning signs that your capacity is getting fuller. Ideally, you want to spot it in the amber zone before you hit the top, so you can stop your cup spilling over.

Use the diagram opposite to identify and write down your personal signs when you are in the red (at risk of overflowing), and the bubbles to spot what happens when you do overflow. Identify your own clues that you are in the green or amber zone and fast approaching red. The amber zone is a sign that you need to think about your capacity and how you can manage it before your cup spills over the edge.

Knowing your capacity level can also help make sense of emotions. It can be confusing, and distressing, to behave in a way that you didn't expect or that is out of character. That time you shouted at your kids for doing something insignificant – it made no sense and you beat yourself up for being a terrible parent. But when you step back and see where your capacity level was at the time, sometimes it all becomes clear. You were at full capacity

because of a stressful day at work, rushing to school pick-up and being on the receiving end of a road-rage incident – teetering at the brim, well into the red zone. As a result, that seemingly innocuous thing that you would have normally dealt with pushed your capacity over the edge. It doesn't change what happened, but by noticing your capacity, you can understand what happened. You will also be more likely to spot the signs and deal with the situation differently next time.

Everyone has individual signs that their cup is near capacity. As you get nearer the top, you may notice your shoulders tightening or have difficulty breathing. Often you can feel stressed, overwhelmed, out of control or find things difficult to deal with. Noticing these signs can be helpful in the quest to understand how full your capacity cup is, so you can take action.

EXERCISE 3

Time to take action

You're grumpy, stressed, overloaded. Well done – you've noticed your amber-zone signs. It looks like you're reaching full capacity. Time to take action. Here are three ways to manage your capacity before your cup overflows and you reach the point of being overwhelmed:

1. Shake it real good

Chuck some things out of your cup. Is there anything in there that can be binned? Are there less taxing alternatives you can do instead? Can you ask someone to help? Sometimes we are reluctant to throw things out as we feel we should be able to manage it all and are failing if we don't. However, chucking things out of your cup is a form of active coping, enabling you to dedicate more resources to the important things.

2. Enough is enough

It's time to say NO. If you are near capacity, try to keep things out of your cup when you can. Before you take on something new, ask yourself if it will push your cup over capacity. If the answer is YES, then the answer is NO to the new thing. Of course, this isn't always possible, and saying no can be hard. But it's an important skill to learn.

3. Doing it for yourself

Taking time for yourself can seem like a waste of precious resources, and you may mistakenly think this will be detrimental to your capacity. A classic example is missing lunch because you have too much on. However, looking after yourself actually increases your capacity, because it lowers your stress and gives you more brain space. Try to take time to encourage good sleeping habits and diet, take regular breaks and do something that makes you feel good, in the knowledge it will better equip you to deal with everything else in your cup and reduce your stress levels.

When life throws rocks at you

In the pathway of life, it's highly unlikely you are going to escape without a few rocks of varying sizes, and with varying impact, being thrown in your direction.

If we have rarely experienced difficult events, we have a tendency to go through life thinking that bad things happen to other people. This means that when difficult things do happen, it is a shock. Meanwhile, people who have faced a difficult situation can be hypervigilant for signs it will happen again. Your past experiences mean your brain is always on the look-out for this, in a bid to protect you. However, when stressful and difficult life events do occur, tough emotions tend to arise, as you try to make sense of things. This is a perfectly normal reaction to what are, hopefully, out of the ordinary life events. Expecting and understanding difficult emotions doesn't necessarily make them easier, because feeling bad feels bad. However, it may help you stop them getting worse.

Stressful life events often bring with them change, to which we have to adapt and adjust. We must learn to navigate a diversion in life's pathway so that we can continue on our new path in the most meaningful and effective way we can. Often, this is not just a change in day-to-day life, but a detour that means our anticipated future is altered, too.

Sometimes difficult events shake us to our very cores, making us question our identities, our coping strategies and sometimes even our guiding beliefs.

Your coping strategies are how you've learnt to manage life so far, and are there to help you navigate the world. They can be a protective layer, cushioning you from the rocks that life throws at you. Sometimes, it's about building up your protective wall and remembering to use this when you need a bit of extra support. At other times, you may find that your coping strategies, which have worked well throughout your life, don't work in the new circumstances and therefore need to be adapted.

Building up your protective wall

Stress can be overwhelming and make you want to hide away under a rock. In fact, hiding under a rock (or preferably under a cosy blanket) may be the right coping strategy to use sometimes, for example when you are at full capacity and just need some relaxation. But at other times, hiding away adds to your stress as it means you stop using and benefitting from your coping strategies. At these times, it's worth considering if the short-term discomfort and effort needed to get out from under your 'rock' might be more helpful for you than staying put.

Sometimes life gets in the way of being able to fully utilize your coping strategies. You may need to think of half-way alternatives, so you can still feel the positive effects without as much investment. If you know that exercise makes you feel good but you can't face going to the gym, try a brief walk instead. You like speaking to friends, but can't face seeing them right now – could you meet one trusted friend or have a WhatsApp exchange instead? One of the best ways to employ coping strategies is by thinking flexibly about whether you could still gain some benefit by applying them in a slightly different way.

Think about and write down what's in your protective cushioning wall. What coping strategies do you use to reduce the impact of stressful life events? You can refer to this at times of feeling overwhelmed as a reminder to make use of your coping tools.

Untangle Your Brain

Untangle your brain: identifying your feelings

When you are going through a major life event, your capacity cup can fill quickly to the point of overwhelm. At this stage your emotions can feel like one big tangled ball of wool. Your brain feels jumbled and muddled, and you can experience intense emotions and bodily sensations, which can make you feel frozen, overstimulated or numb. You don't have space to take a step back and reflect, so things can feel out of control, and you can beat yourself up for feeling bad, rather than recognizing that it's a natural response. All this tends to make you feel worse, when it would be better to recognize and validate your emotions, and be kinder to yourself at a stressful period in life.

Try this brain tangle exercise to start making sense of what you are feeling and why. We are not trying to get rid of emotions: the aim is to recognize them and factors contributing to them. It's also about stepping back and seeing all this in the context of an external life event, rather than internalizing it to mean something about you or blaming yourself.

1. Use the illustration opposite to write down anything that is going through your mind and taking up brain space. It can be a feeling, thought, worry or simply day-to-day tasks. Write one of these at the end of each string. This is a brain dump, getting everything that is in your brain onto paper. So write anything and everything that comes to mind.

2. Once you know what's in your brain, it can be easier to know how to tackle it. You may come up with some ideas about small next steps you can take. It may also direct you towards other tools in this book that will help. However, the main aim is to put words to how you are feeling and be able to articulate the tangle in your mind.

Up your game

When we are stressed and overwhelmed, we can get into a state of high anxiety that makes us feel frozen. As a result, we often stop looking after ourselves – we don't make lunch or take breaks, we stop doing things we enjoy. We are also more likely to resort to quick fixes: drinking more coffee, or drinking more alcohol than usual; we eat more and may crave sweet things or carbs for the energy boost; we hit the easily accessible online-shopping 'buy' button. None of these are inherently bad and may give short-term relief, and that's okay. But sometimes, in the longer term, they can make things worse if we come to rely on them, so developing more sustainable fixes is a good idea.

Even though it may feel like a bad use of your time, if you up your game in looking after yourself at times of high stress, then it can actually increase your capacity just that little bit and help you get through a difficult time. At the very least, it is something you can do that is in your control; so *don't* skip breakfast, make it the night before. Pack a water bottle to take the next day. Take time for a

Buoys to help in choppy water

15-minute walk at lunchtime. Go back to basics and nurture yourself. These small things have incremental, lasting gains. They will not take away the difficult emotions or the stressful situation but they can be protective factors that stop a downward spiral and help support and protect you. I like to think of them as buoys in the water, which hold you up, stop you sinking further and help you navigate a difficult time.

Think about how you can better look after yourself. It may be that some helpful habits have been dropped, or that you have slipped into less helpful ones due to high levels of stress or overwhelm. Write in each buoy a small, easily manageable step that helps you to stay afloat.

EMOTIONS are....

Chapter 3
You, Your Brain and Your Emotions

Experiencing emotions and understanding our experiences in emotional terms is what makes us human. Whoever you are, wherever you are and whatever you are doing, emotions come along with you on the ride and, in fact, they can often direct the ride and make it what it is. Emotions are with you through the best parts of life, helping you reach the euphoric highs and bask in glory. But they are also with you at the worst parts of life, touching your life with sadness, grief and longing. Sometimes, emotions are welcome guests, making you feel fantastic, helping you enjoy the good points and shielding you from risk. At other times, you may wish they would just go away and leave you alone. Emotions are inevitable, changeable, sometimes unpredictable, messy and complex, but are an intrinsic part of us. This chapter delves into what emotions are and introduces a framework for understanding your own emotions and how you respond to them.

EMOTIONS (JUST SOME) *

Perturbed

Elated

Bashful

Shocked

Schadenfreude

Flabbergasted

Crestfallen

Bemused

Horrified

Delighted

Discombobulated

Furious

Perplexed

Amazed

Curious

Envious

* cos I couldn't fit thousands onto the pag

What's the point of those pesky emotions?

So we all experience emotions and it's an inevitable part of being human. But why is the brain designed to have these pesky emotions that can cause so much discomfort and pain? By understanding how emotions work, you can start to interpret your own and use this knowledge to help look after yourself.

First, let's address a myth: if anyone tells you that emotions are all in the mind, they are wrong. Emotions are in the body too – at the root of emotions are feelings, physiological body sensations. That lump in your throat, warmth in your heart, heat rising in your neck – you are not imagining it, these are real physical sensations. So emotions are feelings, sensations in your body; but not all feelings are emotions.

Inside, your body is in perpetual motion, meaning that bodily sensations, or feelings, fluctuate in intensity. Brain and body work in tandem, communicating to allow you to sleep, eat, heal wounds, use energy effectively and respond to your environment. Your brain detects and interprets sensations from your body to enable you to do this. Your brain also creates sensations as it tries to predict your needs, to keep your body in balance – homeostasis – so you function well.

You are only consciously aware of some of these sensations, particularly big spikes of activity, and how they make you feel. Some of these sensations indicate hunger, pain, needing the toilet, being full. Some sensations feel pleasant, others unpleasant; some calming, some arousing. When you do notice them, your brain tries to understand them so that it knows what to do. Is it hunger, thirst, pain, love, worry? Your brain is effectively saying, 'What on earth is going on in that body of yours, and what do I need to do about it?'. So your brain is perpetually responding to feelings, and some of these feelings we label as emotions.

Emotions are constructs we use to understand and conceptualize some of our internal sensations and how they make us feel. Naming an emotion and understanding it allows you to bring it into your consciousness, step back and look at it, creating a buffer between you and those physical sensations that allows you to reflect and respond. So emotions are not all in the mind, but made sense of by the mind. Not so much mind over matter, but mind understanding matter.

Emotions are central to your brain's functioning, to aid decision-making, memory, language, building relationships, communicating with and understanding others. Sometimes we label these as positive or negative, depending on how we feel, but they are simply your brain's way of trying to make sense of the sensory world in which you live. While you may try to ignore those feelings that make you shake, crumble, freeze and stumble, understanding your emotions allows you to regulate them, know what to do about them and create other more helpful feelings. It allows you to ride on top of the wave of emotions, rather than be caught in the wave and dragged along by it.

The brain isn't perfect – in its quest for seeing patterns and responding quickly, sometimes it gets things wrong. Emotions can drive our behaviour, sometimes in an unhelpful direction. So emotions can be tough, but the wonderful thing about them is their path isn't inevitable. They are willing students eager to learn (although sometimes they can take their time), and you can influence your emotions and how you respond to them.

The aim of these exercises, therefore, is not to get rid of emotions, because the more you try to bottle them up and push them away, the more they tend to jump out unexpectedly. The aim is to understand emotions, see them as clues to what is going on, to recognize when they occur and think about how we can most helpfully respond to them and use them to reach our goals.

The emotions thermometer

We don't notice all changes in our body sensations – spikes in feeling are more likely to come to our attention, as they are like a loud noise that enters our awareness quickly. By increasing awareness of how we feel at certain points, we can start to understand our feelings and associated emotions more, which allows us to become better at knowing what to do about them.

Use the emotions thermometer opposite to help you notice and think about how you are feeling and how intense this is. Think about either the physical sensations or you can try to name the emotions (the next exercise on page 68 can be used in tandem to help with this). The higher up the thermometer the more intense the feeling. Note the intensity on the scale.

Emotions fluctuate throughout the day, never mind year, so try to monitor how you are feeling at several points during a single day, or reflect on your whole day afterwards and how it made you feel. You can also refer to the thermometer to help understand how you are feeling at a particular point in time, which can be especially useful when you are feeling overwhelmed or have big feelings you want to make sense of.

Emotions Thermometer

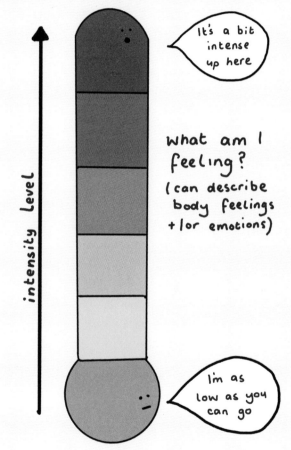

Name that emotion

The more you are aware of and understand your emotions, the more you are able to regulate and respond to them helpfully. The concept 'emotional granulation' is about how finely you can grain, or define and understand, your emotions. It's about developing an emotional vocabulary beyond the basic good/bad, happy/sad, so you can more accurately describe and understand how you feel. Naming an emotion, creating a concept for your feeling, helps to understand it and creates a buffer that allows you to be separate from it, rather than be defined by it.

So, let's play a game of 'name that emotion'. Using the illustration at the start of this topic (see page 62) as a starting point, write down any emotions you feel. You can do this at any time, but it may be particularly helpful when experiencing big or difficult-to-understand emotions. Use any terms you want – words you know, ones you've heard, or ones you make up to describe how you are feeling as accurately as possible. Remember, though, emotions don't come in isolation – you can feel lots of different things at the same time. Use these prompts to guide you:

How do I feel?

What is this emotion telling me about my needs right now?

What can I do to meet these needs?

How can I respond helpfully to this emotion?

Four steps to tolerating difficult feelings

Feeling bad or stressed is not nice – it can feel scary and threatening – and we can try to get rid of the emotion, shut it down or avoid it. This can be counterproductive, though, because it tends to come out in some other way – nightmares, bodily sensations and even illness. Whether we *want* to feel the feelings or not, they will happen anyway. And somewhat ironically, research suggests that trying to suppress emotions actually creates a greater physiological stress response. Recognizing, naming and understanding emotions, rather than seeing them as terrifying entities we have no control over, helps us deal with them more effectively. This can seem counterintuitive – we need to feel bad to make ourselves feel good? But this is where the evidence is pointing. Being aware of, tolerating and understanding those feelings, rather than bottling them up, helps regulate them far better.

A word of caution: if you have been bottling up difficult feelings for a long time, releasing the cork to think about them can be extremely unsettling and overwhelming. If this is the case for you, consider speaking to someone in a safe space, such as a therapist or counsellor, to help you process these feelings at a pace that is right for you.

The following four steps can help you to shift from struggling with to tolerating difficult feelings:

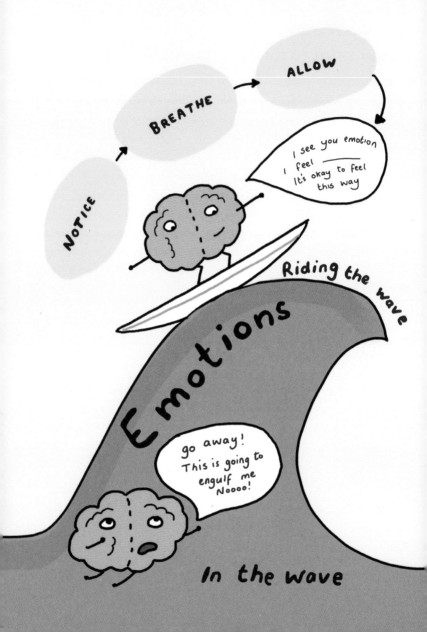

1. **Notice the sensations in your body.** Where are you feeling the emotion? What does it feel like?

⬇

2. **Breathe through the sensation while you continue to observe.** Slow breathing activates your body's rest and relaxation response (see Just Breathe exercise, page 143). Notice if there are any fluctuations or changes in sensation.

⬇

3. **Allow the sensation to be there.** Don't judge it. If it changes, it changes; if not, that's okay. This is about observing and allowing the feeling, rather than ignoring it and pushing it away.

⬇

4. **Remind yourself with helpful statements.** Your mind might start to go back to its long-term patterns of judgement or worry about the feeling. Use supportive statements to remind yourself it's okay to feel this way – these are physiological sensations that come and go, as your body and brain try their best to meet your needs.

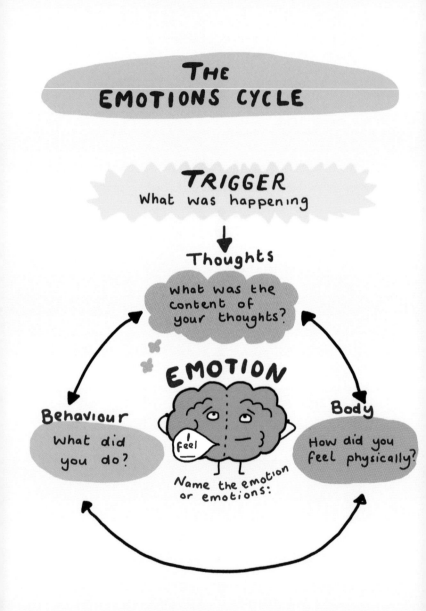

The emotions cycle

When we experience an emotion we respond to it, even if that's by choosing to not respond to it. How we respond is important, as it can help our experience of emotions, or, conversely, it can create unhelpful cycles that are detrimental to our minds. Here we'll look at how emotions affect you and how your responses affect your emotions, using the emotions cycle.

How we feel fluctuates throughout the day, week and year. On a daily basis we often feel good, bad and all stages in between. Sometimes we can regulate physical feelings very easily, without being aware we are doing this, and make ourselves feel better. On a basic level, if we feel hungry, we eat. If we feel flat, a caffeine lift is desperately required. We also regulate how we are feeling psychologically, our emotions. If we feel bored, we might take a break or do something more interesting. If we feel stressed after a long day of work, we might sit on the sofa, switch on a brilliant box set and relax. In all these situations, we are recognizing how we are feeling, identifying something needs to change and doing something to help regulate or change it.

When we notice our emotions we respond to them – sometimes actively, sometimes passively, or by trying to ignore them. Our responses are important to understand as they can have helpful or unhelpful consequences. We may also respond automatically without even noticing and fall into repeating patterns of behaviour. Sometimes it's difficult either to identify that an emotion needs regulating or to know how best to regulate it.

Use the emotions cycle on page 72 to help understand how emotions affect what you think, feel (bodily sensations) and do. You can also use it to think about how you respond to your emotions – targeting thinking, feelings and behaviours – and whether your responses are helpful. This can be difficult to work out, as sometimes things make us feel great in the short-term, like eating a multipack of crisps (yes, I'm talking about myself here), but in the longer-term make us feel worse. Using this framework can help make sense of the emotions themselves, how you are responding, and help you identify and think about other helpful ways to respond.

Using the emotions cycle

Broadly speaking, your responses to your emotions can either create a helpful or unhelpful emotions cycle. Understanding your cycle allows you to identify when it's unhelpful and prompts you to think of other ways to respond. Use the diagram on page 76 and the steps below to establish your emotions cycle and your responses – did they lead you to an emotional dead end, where you got stuck on the emotion, or did they help you find routes to respond to your emotions helpfully?

Step 1
Identify the emotions (and the trigger)
First, use the emotions cycle to answer 'How am I feeling?'. You can use any terms you want. Crappy. Sad. Bad. Pressure, because you've picked the film for tonight, or worry, in case other people won't like it. You can use any emotional descriptors you want, because how you feel is individual to you. Pop this in the centre of the diagram. Remember: there is no right way or wrong way to feel. How you feel is how you feel. We are not aiming to get rid of emotions, as we know we need them. We are aiming to identify them so we can understand how to respond to them.

If you can identify what set the feeling off, that's great – write it down. If not, don't worry – we can't always identify triggers easily for our emotions, and we'll discuss this further later (see Trigger Unhappy, pages 92–9).

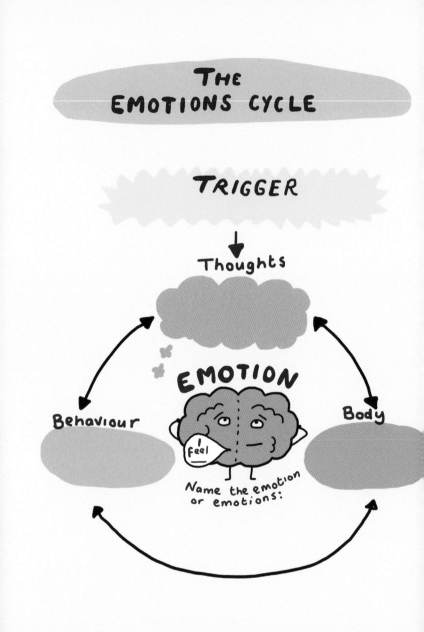

Step 2
Thought – identify what you were thinking

Did you identify a trigger for your emotion? Did looking at Instagram make you feel that other people have it more together than you? Bingo, you've identified your trigger, the Instagram post, and your thought, 'other people are more together than me'. This might have led to other thoughts such as 'Why can I never do anything right?'. Write down as many thoughts as you want.

Step 3
Body – how do your emotions affect your body?

Now you've identified your emotions, think about how you feel in your body. Write down what you are feeling internally. Is your face flushed? Is your heart pounding?

Step 4
Behaviour – think about what you did

Note down your response to the emotion. Did you continue to look at Instagram, meaning that the feelings continued to affect you? Or did you decide to do something else which made you feel better?

Step 5
How helpful were your responses?

Finally, try to consider if your responses from step 4 were helpful, or did they create an unhelpful cycle that made you feel worse? How we respond to our emotions can mitigate the effects they have on our lives: we can regulate the emotions we experience and even create other emotions that break the cycle.

Shame on you, emotions!

Poor emotions, they get a bad press. We tell them off for happening, and shame them, and ourselves, for experiencing them. Yet emotions are an intrinsic part of having a brain and being human; it's like telling off a plant for growing, an animal for eating or a bird for flying. We're berating our brains for doing what they've evolved to do. We're telling ourselves off for an essential function that we require to live. And that's a bit silly, isn't it?

Part of the problem with emotions are not the emotions themselves, but how we respond to them. On top of already feeling rubbish, we add to our discomfort by criticizing ourselves for feeling this way. We create a negative spiral, so that unpleasant emotions create unpleasant emotions that create unpleasant emotions – a cycle, much like one of those concave mirrors, that goes on forever. As if it's not bad enough to feel bad, we make ourselves feel even worse for feeling bad, which then makes us feel even more bad.

We don't have to look back far in history to understand why emotions get a bad press – even in recent times, mental health conditions were sometimes poorly understood, and treatment was often difficult to access and could even be punitive. Shadows of the past don't disappear quickly. They linger and continue to affect our attitudes towards emotions and mental health today, at both a societal and individual level. There is still a lot of stigma directed at mental health and experiencing emotions. As individuals, we fuse these cultural beliefs into our own beliefs, which affect our attitudes to emotions and mental health, and how we respond to our own emotions.

We tell ourselves off for how we feel: 'You are not just sad, you are pathetic for feeling sad.' 'You are not just anxious, you are not normal.' We undermine how we are feeling: 'I'm not feeling bad, I'm just putting it on.' We think having emotions means we are not coping, we are stupid, we are useless, when often it means we are feeling distressed because of a distressing situation. Sometimes our brains even cunningly disguise criticism, to appear helpful or motivational: 'I just need to give myself a kick', 'Get over it', 'Sort yourself out'; but underneath the helpful veneer we continue to invalidate our emotions and ourselves for feeling them.

I frequently hear these types of comments, and sometimes the work I do focuses on how we interpret our own emotions as a threat, or as something inherently wrong with us. As a result, we trigger a cascade of feelings and emotion that makes us feel worse.

What meaning are you giving to your emotions?

Next time you are feeling bad, whatever that emotion may be, take the time to stop and notice it. Use the tools in the emotions cycle (see pages 72-7) to help understand and define the emotion. Now, let's take it further: think about what meaning you are giving to that emotion. Are you criticizing yourself for having it? Are you saying you shouldn't feel this way? Are you saying this is not normal?

Think about how this interpretation of your emotions is making you feel. Is it exacerbating the initial emotions, making you feel worse? If so, you've just spotted the start of that spiral, when one emotion triggers more emotion, and then more emotions, times infinity.

These thought patterns can be so fleeting, or have been so integral to your emotional experience for a long time, that they can be difficult to tease out. Spotting them and pulling them out from their hiding place in your brain is worth the effort, as when you know they are there, you can do something about them. You can use this knowledge to diffuse their power and start to build different ways to respond.

Standing your thoughts in the spotlight and choosing your dance partner

You've identified that critical interpretation of your emotions in Exercise 1 and have it exposed in the spotlight of your attention. In the illustration, note this down in the top thought bubble.

By placing your interpretation in the spotlight and standing back from it, you can start to remove the thought's power. You don't have to actively engage with it, believe it or let it be your tango partner, simply because it is there. Instead, you can recognize it for what it is: a thought not a fact. You might even have a little laugh with it and agree to have different viewpoints. The thought is more likely to accept this than if you try to ignore it completely, because I can pretty much guarantee that if you try *not* to think about something, you will end up thinking about it more.

Once these thoughts lose their power and start to shrink, they can leave a gap in your spotlight. You can fill this gap, based on an objective stance on the situation. Choose those thoughts that you will engage with and trust to be your tango partner, those which will enable you to respond helpfully to your emotions. Put these in the bottom thought bubble. Here are some ideas to tell yourself when you experience emotions:

It's okay to feel this way.

Emotions are a normal part of being human.

Having emotions is not a sign of weakness.

THE ANATOMY OF ANXIETY

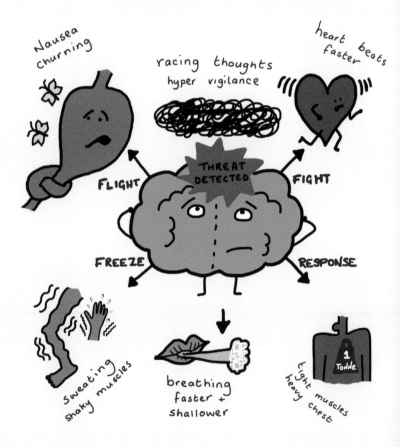

Anxiety alert

Anxiety is an emotion that has a powerful effect on life, as it is intrinsically linked to stress, which is an almost inevitable part of life, and is associated with a key body system that we need to help us survive – the sympathetic nervous system. I've always thought this was wrongly named, as it didn't seem very sympathetic to me. What's so sympathetic about a system that produces all these unpleasant sensations in our bodies – clammy hands, churning stomach, tense muscles, shortness of breath? It's the flight, fight or freeze response that occurs when we have heightened emotions, including stress and anxiety, and our bodies get us ready for action.

As I've grown to know it, I've realized I've misjudged the sympathetic nervous system and it is actually far more sympathetic than I gave it credit for. It is part of the autonomic nervous system, which controls unconscious processes that keep us functioning. It responds to an identified risk or stressor, be it real or imagined (we'll soon find out imagined is just as real as real), by triggering adrenaline and cortisol, which directs our energy to get us ready to deal with the risk appropriately.

Anxiety is one of the emotional concepts with which we most closely associate these sensations (along with other emotions including fear, anger and shock). Like all emotions, what we label as anxiety is not inherently bad; sometimes it can help us muster enough energy and alertness to get us through a situation. For example, your system correctly predicts that you need lots of energy and alertness to speak to that very large and scary audience of psychologists (yes, I'm speaking about myself here!). So actually, it is a considerate and sympathetic system after all, as it keeps you alive and helps you along.

However, sometimes it gets out of balance. Perhaps we over-predict threat because of our past experiences or life is throwing too many rocks at us and we are at the point of being overwhelmed. At these times our sympathetic system is not quite so sympathetic. It's firing on all cylinders, predicting we need energy all the time. We become hyper-vigilant for threat. We avoid doing things because they feel too big and too scary. We have these strong fight or flight physical sensations more than is required, which is unpleasant, and can make us feel distressed. We can't sleep, our eating patterns are disrupted, our thinking becomes muddled, our bowels misbehave, all of which creates more stress. Although our bodies mean well, long-term high levels of stress, cortisol production, and all that that entails, are detrimental to our wellbeing, both physical and mental. Our well-intended body system, which is desperately trying to keep us safe, has become unhelpful to how we function. And that's when anxiety becomes unhelpful and we need to think about how best to intervene.

Completing your anxiety cycle

Using the template of the emotions cycle on page 76, draw a new version for your anxiety cycle.

Step 1
What makes you feel anxious?

Think about what makes you anxious and fill this in the trigger box. Do you feel other emotions at the same time – if so, note them down. Once you think about it, you might start to notice patterns of events that result in anxiety. Some are shared by many people – anxiety about public speaking is extremely common, for example. At other times, your triggers may be your thoughts themselves. Imagined events are just as real to our minds and bodies and, therefore, can have the same effect as real-life events.

Sometimes we can't fully understand our triggers. When things feel out of our control, they feel threatening, so the body system responds to the threat. Sometimes the brain notices patterns in situations that remind us of unpleasant past events, and this creates anxiety. What triggers it can change over time, but understanding what makes you anxious can help you manage it.

Step 2
How do you respond?

Now think about how you respond when you are anxious and complete the remaining boxes in the anxiety cycle. Here are some general ways people respond when anxious. However, everyone's patterns will be distinct, and will vary in different situations.

Body Your heart beats faster to pump more oxygen around your body. The blood flows to your hands and feet, ready for action. Your lungs work harder and you breathe faster. Your stomach churns as the blood flow is redirected to your extremities.

Thoughts You may predict that terrible things will happen, that what you do will have a negative outcome, or that you will feel horrible. You may also predict that you will not manage or cope with a scenario, that you will fail, or make a fool of yourself. You may ruminate over perceived failures in the past. Or you may criticize yourself for feeling anxious at all.

Actions What do you do when you are anxious? Hide under a rock until it is over? Phone your mum? You might respond with aggression, irritableness or frustration. You may directly target the anxiety, by problem-solving or breathing slowly. Or maybe you try and distract yourself from it by doing something else.

Step 3
Are your responses helpful or unhelpful to how you feel?
Your responses can either keep you circling an anxiety roundabout or help you find routes off it. Think about what keeps the anxiety going and makes you feel worse. What helps manage it and helps you tolerate it? Focus on whether your responses keep you on the anxiety roundabout or help you off it. Listing out the helpful responses and identifying what makes things worse will enable you to get off the roundabout faster the next time you feel anxious.

Chapter 4
What Can Make Us Feel Bad?

Emotions rarely appear out of the blue, although it can often feel like they do. How you feel is inherently linked to your environment, both past and present. Your brain's understanding of and predictions about the world are based on the only information it has, past experience. Therefore, the sensory world and your environment are intrinsically linked to your experience of emotions. Sometimes your emotions are a sign that you need to take action – that something in your environment needs to change. This chapter looks at understanding environmental triggers, whether these are in our control or not, and how and when we can manage them. It also looks at common triggers that we can take action to address.

Trigger unhappy

Many things that happen in life necessarily create or trigger emotions. Important life events, including health concerns, moving house or losing a loved one, can be stressful, and, as a result, big and sometimes difficult emotions are an intrinsic part of these experiences. At these times, emotions are a sign that we need to look after ourselves. Other stressful life events, such as work pressure, bullying or being too busy, create emotions that are signs that something in our environment needs to change.

Identifying a trigger can help you decide the best way to respond to your emotion. Is it a normal response to a difficult life event? Is it a sign that you need to take action, to change the thing causing stress? Do you need to build up your coping skills to help you manage the situation? Do you need to tackle the trigger itself or your responses to it? Using the emotions cycle (see pages 72–7) can help you identify whether there is a clear trigger and think about what you can do about it.

A trigger implies that something in the environment has changed and resulted in the emotion. For example, you may hate dogs, and seeing a preened poodle as you left your house that morning has caused you to feel anxious (or perhaps irritated at the ridiculousness of putting a pink bow on a dog). In this instance, the poodle (and your beliefs about dogs) was the trigger that resulted in your emotional response. Or, a clear life event may have impacted how you are feeling longer term.

At other times the trigger may not be so clear. There may have been lots of little things going on, adding to your capacity cup (see pages 44–51). A thought may have popped into your head and created an emotional response. You may have noticed this, but sometimes fleeting thoughts can be gone before you've even spotted them. In addition, it can be the cumulative effects of hunger, frustration and tiredness that make us feel bad.

When we look for triggers it can sometimes be hard to identify anything at all. This can be annoying, as we like certainty in our complex world, but not knowing is okay too – sometimes emotions just arise. While it's great to understand when there is a trigger, it's even more important to notice the emotion. If you can identify a cause that's great, but if not, you can still think about how you respond.

Identifying triggers

When you experience emotions, use the emotions cycle (see pages 72-7) to try and identify what has triggered them. It may have been one event, or it may have been a build-up of events, creating stress and overwhelm. If the latter, use the capacity cup (see pages 44-51) to help identify gradual build-ups affecting stress levels. When it is hard to recognize a trigger, it may be helpful to consider these factors:

Have you been eating and drinking properly?

Are you sleeping well and resting enough?

Is there anything creating additional stress in your life right now?

Have there been any changes in your life recently?

Has a memory of a past experience triggered your feelings?

If you can't identify a trigger, that's okay. Continually searching for a reason when there is none apparent can get you stuck on an emotion rather than thinking of how you can respond. So don't search too hard for a trigger; instead, accept this is how you feel, and shift your focus to how you can respond helpfully.

Can I change the trigger?

Understanding your triggers can help you decide whether you should be targeting the trigger directly to change it, whether you need to think about how you respond to it (using your emotions cycle, see pages 72–7) or do both at the same time. This can be thought about in the following terms:

Clear triggers that can be changed

If there is a clear, identifiable trigger that can be changed, then your resources are best targeted at the trigger itself. For example, if overusing your phone makes you feel bad, then put limits on your phone use. However, sometimes the solutions are more difficult. For example, if you are experiencing bullying in the workplace, while this trigger needs addressing, the solutions may take time. You have identified that you need to take action to change a real threat, but you also need to build up your coping strategies to manage this stressful trigger and target your responses at the same time.

Clear triggers that can't be changed

Some life events result in big emotions that can't be changed – for example, the death of a loved one or coping with a difficult life event, such as being made redundant. In these scenarios it's important to look after yourself and boost your coping strategies as best you can. Try to recognize your emotions, think about what you can do to help you get through and target what you can control – for example, using the Tolerating Uncertainty exercise in the Catastrophe topic (see pages 178–9).

If you're not sure if the trigger or your responses need to be targeted

Sometimes you may find something difficult that could potentially be changed and decide you want to overcome it. If you are anxious about public speaking but want to be able to do it, you need to target your emotions response cycle to help enable you to do this. At other times, though, it is harder to work out what to target – the trigger or how you respond to it. If you get anxious in busy shops, you can order your food online or go shopping at a quieter time. This is targeting the trigger, and that's okay. However, you may decide you want to be comfortable going to busy shops, in which case you will target your responses (thoughts, behaviours and body) in the emotions cycle, to help you cope with the trigger. There's not always a correct answer: sometimes it's a case of managing the trigger to reduce stress; sometimes you need to change your response; or it can be a mixture of both. It's about working out what is most helpful to you at the current time.

Targeting the trigger is sometimes unhelpful. You might stop going out and seeing people because it makes you anxious, but actually you benefit from seeing friends, so targeting the trigger by avoiding it has an overall negative impact on your life here.

Identifying where to target your energy and response can be difficult, and no one can possibly make this judgement call correctly all the time. Keeping an eye on your emotions cycle and thinking if your response has had an overall beneficial or detrimental impact on your life will help.

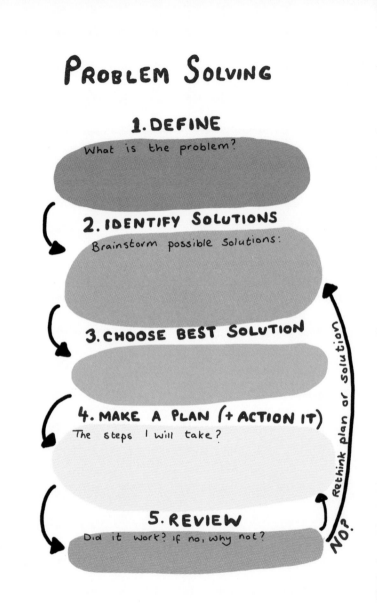

Problem-solving triggers that need to be changed

If you've identified that something about a trigger needs to change, it can be helpful to take some time to think about how best to do that. Triggers that need changing can often seem overwhelming, so this exercise can help you face up to them and find helpful ways to move forward.

Use the diagram opposite to work out how to change a particular trigger. You may find it helpful to talk it through with someone who can provide another perspective on the situation. They may also be able to help find more, or different, creative solutions for how to problem-solve difficult triggers.

It's important to later review whether this solution was successful, and if not go back to the drawing board. And remember: don't beat yourself up if not, you may not get it right first time!

Antisocial media

Love it or loathe it, smart phone and social media use can impact on our mental wellbeing in a number of ways. It can directly affect how we feel, or exacerbate difficult feelings. It can take time away from other activities that we value and are good for us, and it can affect our basic functioning, including sleep. It looks like social media is here to stay, so we have to learn to manage it, and its impact on us, as best we can.

Our phones give us instant access to more information than we've ever had before. This can be fantastic, when you need the number of the local takeaway quickly. However, it can also be a distraction, using up our limited attention and taking our minds away from the actual world in which we live. Constant information can be stressful, and fill your capacity cup. Your phone can be like a toddler mid-tantrum: its perpetual beeps directing you to multiple channels and notifications, all demanding your attention NOW!

Social media is designed to suck us in, and before you know it, 60 minutes have passed. The danger of the endless scroll means we are drawn into a never-ending story, with no chapter breaks, no page turns to make us stop and become aware of what's happening. Research suggests that the more time you spend on social media, the more likely you are to have poor mental health (although it's not clear if this is cause or effect). We seek validation through social media, and not receiving this may impact negatively on us. The feedback we receive, through likes and comments, can make us feel good and is reinforcing, which can be addictive.

There are other potential pitfalls: social media breeds comparison, where we are prone to compare other's curated projections of perfection to our own less than perfect (read 'normal') life. Research has indicated that viewing the often narrow perceptions of body normality on social media can make women, particularly younger women, feel bad about their own bodies (and increasingly this applies to men, too). Putting ourselves on social media opens us up to judgement and criticism from others, which can vary from unintentionally hurtful comments to trolling and bullying.

Of course, social media has positive aspects too. We interact with others, share our creativity, find connections that normalize our experiences, and learn, among other things. It can also provide a welcome distraction, reading material, or a laugh. Looking after your mind is not about rejecting social media; it's about making sure that your social media usage is helpful, and learning to recognize when it starts to become problematic.

Who's in control, you or your phone?

Use this checklist to highlight areas you may need to work on. Tick any that you feel apply to you, and be honest. If you answer 'yes' to any of these questions, it might be time to reassess how you use your phone or social media, to ensure it is a positive influence in your life rather than a hindrance.

Is your phone use making you feel bad?

☐ *Do you feel anxious, sad or inadequate when you scroll, and does this continue afterwards?*

☐ *Do you have time away from your phone?*

☐ *Do you check your social media compulsively?*

☐ *Do you feel compelled to post on social media to get likes?*

☐ *Do you feel bad when you don't get as many likes as you'd hoped for a post?*

☐ *Does your phone use stop you doing what you really want to do?*

☐ *Is your phone use getting in the way of what's important to you, e.g. relationships, hobbies?*

☐ *Does it impact negatively on your real life, including sleep, diet, work, parenting?*

Take back control

If you've identified that your phone or social media use is making you feel bad and stopping you doing what you want to do, it's time to start wrestling back control. Try these strategies:

Put realistic limits on your usage by using apps to set time restrictions or warnings. These tools help you to set proactive limits and boundaries for when it is acceptable to use your phone.

Don't check your phone while in bed.

Curate your social media feed: unfollow or mute people who make you feel bad.

Turn off alerts so that you control when you check social media, rather than it controlling you.

Bear in mind that you are viewing carefully selected images of others.

Be aware of the potential pitfalls of sharing personal information, and make an informed decision about what to post.

Keep your phone in a separate room or switch it off at times that you don't want to use it.

Break the habit – make active decisions

Picking up your phone can become a habit that is difficult to break. Phone use becomes so automatic that you are not always aware you are doing it. However, if you bring your phone use into your awareness, both before you start and while you are using it, you can then make an active decision about what you will do next – will you continue using your phone or not? You can do this in a variety of ways:

Before you pick up your phone: stop and think. Is your phone use right now helpful to you or not? Do you actually want to use your phone for something specific? If not, try to resist the urge.

While you are using your phone: it is easy to be drawn in and lose track of time. The key is to break your attention, so that you become aware of what you are doing. Set an external prompt before you start, such as a timer function on your phone. When the prompt occurs, ask yourself the following questions:

How am I feeling right now?

Is continuing to use my phone helpful or unhelpful to me?

Do I want to continue using it?

If the answer is 'no' to any of these, distract yourself by doing something else that absorbs your attention, or physically move your phone away from you so it isn't easily accessible.

The art of comparison

We all do it, our brains are tuned to do it and social media lends itself perfectly to doing it: comparing ourselves to others. How successful am I compared to my colleagues? How are my parenting skills compared to others? Comparison itself isn't inherently bad, and sometimes it can be helpful, allowing us to navigate the social world effectively, choose supportive allies and partners, and identify where to change. How the comparison makes us feel depends on several factors, including the conclusion we come to from the comparison and the reference point we use. So, if we feel we are performing much worse than our peers, or feel differently to most people, these upward comparisons can make us feel inadequate.

Social media is a breeding ground for comparison. We are bombarded with curated images of other people's lives: unattainable bodies, perfect houses, fun-filled family days out, lifestyles beyond our means. We may know this is not reality, but the result is often upward social comparisons which can make us feel anxious. We feel that we are different or not as good as other people. Frequently these comparisons are invalid, as we are comparing ourselves to someone else's filtered highlight reel, an idealized view. We are only seeing part of the story, and we really shouldn't judge a book, or make comparisons with it, based on two pages from chapter 7.

We don't just compare ourselves to other people; we also compare ourselves and our lives to our imagined selves. We compare our success, failures and current situation to an alternative imagined life, or anticipated future. 'Life would have been better if I'd got that job. I'd be happier if I had more money.' Our simulated version contains none of the bad parts, so it is inevitably going to be a better version that makes our real life or choices look worse than they actually are.

When we make comparisons, we are using a reference point. We can think of these as upward comparisons (comparing ourselves to people we think are doing better) or downward comparisons (comparing ourselves to people we feel are worse off). It might surprise you to learn that research suggests that Olympic bronze-medal winners are usually happier with their achievement than silver-medal winners, despite the latter being a better achievement. This appears to be due to the reference point they use. Silver-medal winners make upward comparisons to the gold medal, so feel they have just missed out on being an Olympic champion, whereas bronze-medal winners make downward comparisons to the rest of the competitors, so feel lucky to get a medal.

The meaning we give to a comparison can make it helpful or unhelpful. Often we assume an attribute makes another person's life better; it means they are a better person than us. They are richer, so life is easier. Their fantastic job makes them happier. We are not as good as them. Not only are these comparisons often invalid, as we base them on incomplete or partial information, the assumptions we make are often just as incorrect. We can't know if they are happier or more fulfilled. So it's not the comparison but the assumptions we make based on it that cause us problems.

Your brain is built to compare, and will likely continue to do it whether you want it to or not. However, you can teach yourself to notice when you are making unfair comparisons. You can guide your mind to question the validity of your judgements and choose more accurate reference points, all of which will help paint a clearer picture.

Notice comparison: how valid is it?

These three steps can help you notice your comparisons and think about how you respond when they happen. Refer to the emotions cycle (see pages 72–7), using your comparison reference point as the trigger, to help you jot down your answers.

1. Notice you are making a comparison

Who or what are you comparing yourself to?

How is this making you feel?

What story did you assume about yourself or the other person when you made the comparison, e.g. they are so much more together than me?

2. Question the validity of the comparison

Are you making a comparison against only partial information, e.g. how someone portrays themselves on social media?

Are you comparing yourself to an idealized imaginary situation, not accounting for all the bad bits?

Are you really comparing like for like? Or are you comparing your harshest criticism of yourself to the best bits of someone else?

Are you making invalid assumptions about people, e.g. they are always happy, and comparing yourself to these?

3. What meaning are you drawing from your comparison?

Are you making unfair judgements about yourself based on your comparison? E.g. I'm not successful; I haven't achieved?

Are you making incorrect assumptions about the other person based on the comparison, e.g. her life must be better as she is prettier than me; she must be happy because she has that job?

Is there actually any proof to back up your assumptions, e.g. there is no evidence that having lots of money or being famous makes you any happier?

Choose your reference point

Where you set your reference point strongly influences a comparison and the meaning you derive from this. Are you making an upward or a downward comparison? Once you know where you are setting your reference point, you can guide your brain to choose another. If you put yourself in the position of the silver medal winner, focus on the bronze winner (a downward comparison), not the gold, and consider the greatness of your achievement. In nearly any situation in life there will be people better and worse than you, and you can have agency in choosing where you set your reference point.

Or you may choose a different reference point altogether. Perhaps it's fairer to compare your silver-winning time to your time in the same race last year. In my work with people in rehab we discuss setting their comparison reference point to the start of rehabilitation rather than prior to illness. Once you are aware of where you have set your reference point, you can recalibrate it to somewhere fairer.

Comparison to an imagined alternative

We do this all the time. We think life would be better if we got that job, we'd be happier if that thing hadn't happened to us, or *when* we achieve X,Y,Z we *will* feel… This is a comparison where we make assumptions about what would happen in an alternative simulation of reality. These simulated versions usually overemphasize the potential positives and underplay the negatives, so this will always be an invalid upward comparison.

Comparing yourself to an idealized alternative can result in many emotions, one of which is regret. Effectively you are comparing a decision you made or what happened to you with something you perceive would have been better. Reality can never win when you compare it to a perfected imaginary version.

Try to remind yourself that you actually have no way of knowing if the alternative would have been better or even any different, and in fact it could have been a far worse outcome. Consider recalibrating your imaginary self-reference point through a technique called negative visualization. Ask yourself, 'What would life be like if I didn't have what I have now?' This can reset your reference point to a downward imaginary comparison, which research shows is more likely to result in gratefulness for what you have and appreciation of the decisions you have made.

IMPOSTER ICEBERGS

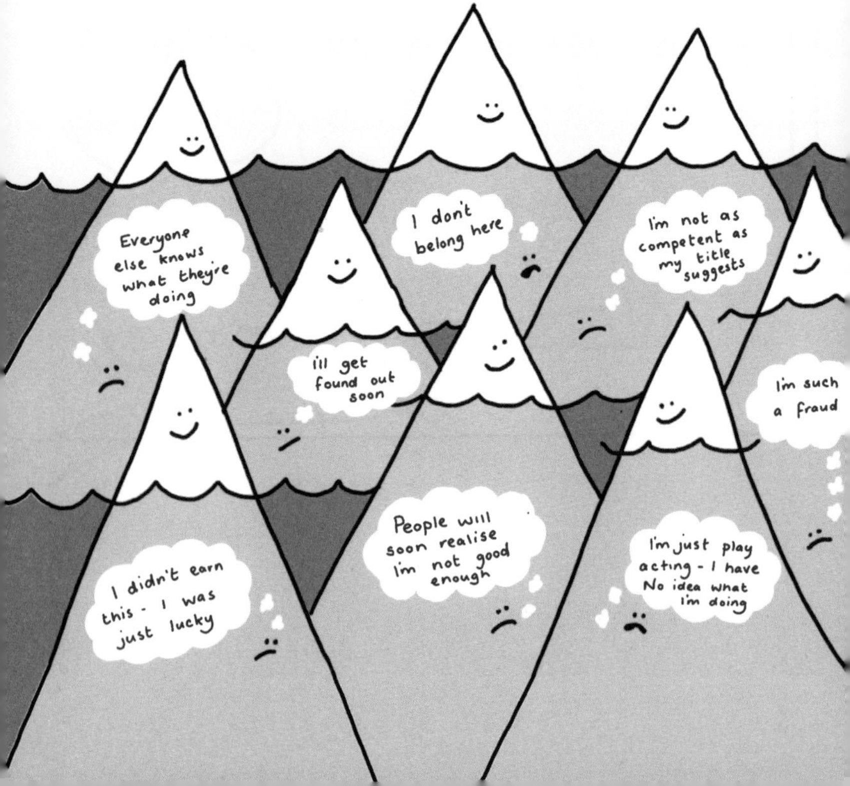

Imposter syndrome

Have you ever wondered when the day will come that you get found out? When people will discover that you don't actually know what you are doing? If you have, then you are not alone. It is estimated that around 70 per cent of people have experienced imposter syndrome. Although not a diagnosis, imposter syndrome describes someone who, despite being competent, believes that their success is down to luck, rather than their own skills and efforts, and that they are not as skilled as they appear.

This results in a fear that someday your underlying lack of knowledge and skills will be exposed. It can cause anxiety, as you are waiting to make the mistake that will ultimately reveal you as a fraudster of epic proportions. Imposter syndrome can stop you going for jobs or promotions, speaking at meetings or even asking for things that would be helpful to you, as your self-doubt gets in the way of believing you can do all these things. This does not just apply to work, you can feel an imposter in just about any area of life, including being a parent, or even just being a grown up!

The irony of imposter syndrome is that it usually occurs in people who do actually know what they are talking about. There are psychological studies, the results of which have been termed the Dunning–Kruger effect, which demonstrate this – often the more competent we are, the less competent we think we are, because we are more aware of how much we don't know.

We can also experience something called the halo effect. This means we band together what we see as positive qualities and make incorrect assumptions about them. If we think somebody is attractive or confident, we assume they have other positive qualities such as competence, even if that's not the case. In imposter syndrome we can apply the inverse to ourselves – if we are not confident, surely this means we are not competent – but this is not true.

Another factor in imposter syndrome is where we look to for reasons – we tend to attribute negative events to internal causes, and positive events to external causes. This means that anything bad that happens is clearly because we are rubbish, and, conversely, we can never take responsibility or give ourselves credit for any of the good stuff.

Feelings of anxiety or self-doubt can lead us to incorrect assumptions about ourselves: 'I feel anxious, therefore I must be doing something wrong.' Actually, you may simply feel anxious, because you are in unknown territory or balancing lots of complex information. Having and managing self-doubt is not abnormal; in fact, it can keep you in check and highlight when you need more learning or information.

Recognizing self-doubt and discomfort

Self-doubt is at the heart of imposter syndrome. We all have varying degrees of it, but it's important to recognize when this tips over into unhelpfulness, as this means you need to think about which actions you can take to manage it.

While this isn't a scientifically validated scale, I've used the drawing below in my clinical work to help people recognize when they are feeling self-doubt and consider how best to manage it. Think about where you are on the scales in the diagram. This will vary according to what else is going on in your life, and the fullness of your capacity cup (see pages 44–51).

Where is your self-doubt right now? Is it helpful and keeping you in check, identifying and encouraging you to learn new information and seek support when necessary? Or has it tipped towards unhelpful, or even approaching a crippling stage, stopping you doing things, leading you to feel ashamed?

Managing self-doubt

So, you think your self-doubt has tipped into being unhelpful.
Or perhaps you just want to manage the self-doubt associated
with imposter syndrome generally? These five steps will help you
to identify what has triggered this specific episode of imposter
syndrome and think about how you can manage it.

1. Identify – recognize the reasons for feeling this way.
• Are there any specific triggers? If so, can you do anything about
these right now?

• Are you facing uncertainty, e.g. are you in a new role?

• Are your stress levels high?

• Do you have too much to do?

• Do you need additional skills for what you have been asked
to do?

There may be no clear trigger, and that's okay!

2. Take stock – notice how you are feeling.
• Describe the physiological sensations.

• Describe the emotions.

• Describe your thoughts.

Use the emotions cycle (see pages 72–7) to help with this.

3. Normalize - feeling like an imposter is common.

• Remind yourself this is just a physiological feeling. This is simply your body getting you ready for action.

• It is normal to feel some discomfort, even more so when working in uncertainty or doing something new.

• Remind yourself that it's okay to feel this way. Most people feel this way at some point. Many people you admire, who look outwardly confident, will feel this way too.

4. Reframe - this feeling does not reflect your competence.

• Having a thought doesn't make it a fact.

• Remind yourself of similar times in the past you have managed.

• Self-doubt isn't all bad – sometimes it can be helpful to self-assess and be open-minded to other views.

5. Problem-solve - next steps to feeling better.

• Remind yourself of your achievements.

• Are there any practical steps you can take to target the triggers?

• Tell someone you trust – sharing your thoughts can be extremely validating, and it's likely your confidant will identify with this too!

• Are there practical steps you can take to manage this, such as talking through your uncertainties at work with a mentor?

• Seek a trusted external view on your performance – does your view match external perceptions?

Keep your attributions in check

When you experience imposter syndrome, bad things are internalized, so they are all your fault, and good things are externalized, so you can never take credit for them. By spotting the causes you assign to events you can look at this in a more rational way, pull apart that attribution and think about the real causes.

Use the diagram opposite to help with this. When you spot yourself making an attribution, fill in the top balloons to determine where you are assigning cause. For example, are you blaming yourself 100 per cent for a mistake that happened (an internal cause)? Or giving yourself no credit for a positive outcome? Now step back and use the bottom balloons to think about the actual causes. Did other external factors contribute to this mistake? Did you have more influence or impact on that positive outcome than you are giving yourself credit for?

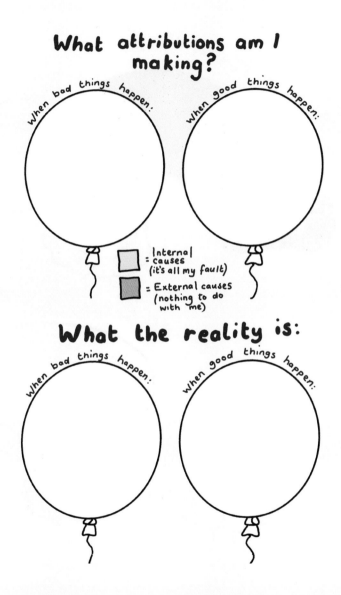

You reserve the right to fail

Okay, so your brain has lots of shortcuts, biases and loopholes that make it a rapid but imperfect consumer of information. Yet you can learn a lot from your brain, especially how it deals with its own mistakes. The brain works through the process of prediction and revision. It determines what it thinks will happen, and if it makes an incorrect prediction it recalibrates to account for this information. It builds upon lots of instances of difference to provide as wide and accurate an understanding of the world as possible. What a clever thing it is – it knows it needs to predict things incorrectly to learn something new. I think that's amazing. If only we could apply this understanding to our conscious mind.

The fear of mistakes and, in its extreme form, perfectionism, are common – as humans we are driven to achieve goals, we like to do things well and we don't like getting things wrong. Society rewards perfectionism and achievement to the extent that we start to think this defines us or makes us happy. We are also social animals that like to be viewed positively by others, so we like to do well. Making mistakes and perceived failures, on the other hand, can result in unpleasant feelings. If we are not 'on top of everything' – work, life, kids, marriage, healthy home-cooked meals – then we think we are failing. Nothing less than perfect is failure;

feeling overwhelmed is failure, feeling like you are not managing is failure. It's all about us; *we* are not coping, *we* are not good enough. It's back to those attributions (see pages 120–1) – we internalize the causes, blame ourselves and fail to recognize that this is a perfectly normal, universal experience.

This aversion to mistakes is in direct contrast with the reality of life, which is inevitably full of failures, whether through our own mistakes or no fault of our own. Wherever the responsibility lies, it turns out that life satisfaction is not linked to how much goes *right* in life, but in learning to manage when things go *wrong*. Tolerating and allowing mistakes helps reduce stress levels and makes us happier.

Those things we think of as the biggest failures can often turn out in retrospect to be positive pivotal points, leading us down another path, making us take stock, learn new skills or have new ideas. It may seem unbearable at the time, but long term we are often grateful for these 'failures'. Many successes arise from perceived mistakes and diversions, and people report that their resilience in the face of adversity is the key to their success. So what we define as a failure may turn out to be anything but.

Referring to the emotions cycle (see pages 72–7), it's not hard to see how fearing mistakes or failures can impact on our behaviour. We can end up avoiding doing things we are not good at or shying away from learning new skills, as not getting things right first time feels uncomfortable (this is also tied into imposter syndrome, see pages 114–21). Our fear of mistakes means we can procrastinate until either we are sure we can do something perfectly, or (in the case of my essay deadlines at university) we've left it so late we no longer have a choice or luxury of time. We can be driven to continue to seek perfection, as reaching goals and success creates positive feelings, which reinforces this behaviour. This is tied into mistakenly believing that our achievements define us.

In life, while mistakes and failures are inevitable, how we respond to them is not inevitable, and learning to accept them is extremely good for our mental health and our minds.

The real meaning of mistakes

Consider the meaning that you are placing on your perceived mistakes, and then reframe this more objectively. Do your mistakes really mean what you think they do? Think about what is a more accurate story.

What stories are you telling yourself about mistakes?

Are you telling yourself that you 'always get things wrong'?

Do you tell yourself you are useless because you made a mistake?

Do you think that other people will think you are incompetent?

Are you telling yourself you are not coping, when life has thrown some rocks at you that anyone would have difficulty with?

Are you magnifying your mistakes to be far bigger and mean more about you than they actually do?

What is the actual meaning of your mistakes?

What would you tell a colleague or friend if they made this mistake? Often we are more objective when we look at scenarios in other people's lives.

What do you think about people who own up to their mistakes and take steps to address them?

Is the reality that making mistakes is human?

Does a mistake really define you?

Does dealing with these hurdles actually help you in some way?

Befriend your mistakes

A life without stumbling blocks and failures only exists in fairy tales. I'm not saying you're going to like those mistakes – or the uncomfortable emotions they create – but give yourself permission to fail. Befriend your mistakes, so they don't terrify you, and see them as acquaintances you can tolerate and accept.

When you do need to learn from your mistakes (because we all do at times), then approach them with an open mind, rather than shaming yourself and wanting to run away and hide. It can be helpful to have some key phrases to transform mistakes from the monsters they feel like to the more diminutive creatures they actually are. This illustration gives some ideas for this and how to rethink your perception of mistakes. Add your own phrases or statements to those suggested below.

Shrinking the Mistake Monster

One mistake doesn't mean I'm a failure.
mistakes don't define me.
Everybody makes mistakes.
Mistakes are part of life.
I'm allowed to get things wrong.

The great attention shift

By directing you to your next steps, detecting errors on the way and highlighting risks, your brain tries to navigate you towards your goals. Add in perfectionism and a fear of mistakes, and this can make you overly vigilant for any mistakes you make. It may even lead you to label actions as mistakes when they aren't. As a consequence, your brain forgets to pause, reflect and acknowledge those steps already completed – your achievements. You overlook the good in favour of setting targets and noticing the bad.

However, you can give your brain a little nudge in the right direction. Use the 'Ta Da' list opposite to record things you have done well. Achievements don't need to be big – getting out of bed despite feeling rubbish is an achievement. Staying calm when the kids are fighting, that's an achievement, as is allowing yourself some time to do something you enjoy. These are all our little daily 'ta das'.

This is a seemingly simple task, but one that gives you recognition for what you have done, directing attention to your achievements rather than passing them by. This can shift your perspective in a more positive way, helping you to notice and remember your successes in both the short- and long-term.

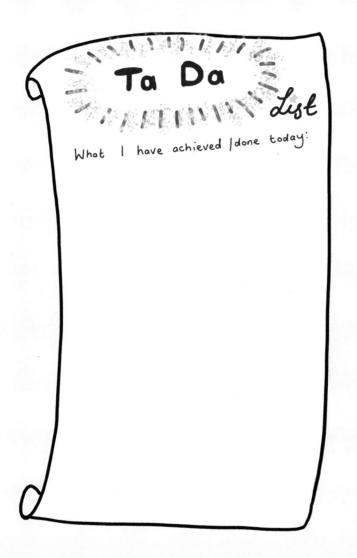

Ta Da List

What I have achieved/done today:

Chapter 5

Responding to Emotions – What We Do

Our behaviours are central to looking after our minds, as they have a knock-on effect on our thoughts, beliefs and emotions. This can be the case in both the short- and long-term. Our actions, such as going outside for a walk, can have an immediate impact by changing our thoughts or physiological responses and, therefore, how we feel. We already know that creating and maintaining social relationships is one of the strongest predictors of positive mental and physical health. When we break this down, our relationships are ultimately developed and defined by our actions. Will we pick up the phone to speak to that friend? Decide to talk through what's troubling us or them? Do something helpful for other people? What we do builds these social relationships. In the same way, on a wider scale, what we do builds our lives in a way that is ultimately helpful to our minds, or not. Looking after your mind is about creating habits that you can keep doing in your life. This chapter focuses on fostering behaviours that are positive to your mind and body.

Change and goals

Anything you choose to try as a result of reading this book will create a change, whether it's putting in place a new behaviour, trying a new activity or working with your thoughts. Change isn't always easy – it can take a lot of effort to initiate and maintain. To illustrate this, I'd like to introduce you to the band of 85 billion neurons in your brain.

Your band of neurons are singing to each other and making connections all the time. Some songs are louder than others: the ones we've been singing longest; the voices from childhood that still fill our heads; the lifelong patterns of behaviours; the habits that come naturally; and the thoughts whose origins we can't even remember. Each of these is a song our neurons are singing, by connecting and making a neural pathway. And they've been going along these pathways for a long time, so they are easy routes to take.

Any time we try something new, we are asking some of those 85 billion neurons to deviate from their well-worn path and create a new path, and that takes effort and time. For example, when we decide to try a new behaviour, like taking a walk at lunchtime, or change a current behaviour, like eating fruit instead of snacking on crisps, it not only requires you to inhibit your automatic response, but also to almost consciously have to create a new pathway.

I often use the neural pathway analogy when talking about changing thoughts or behaviours. Your neurons automatically follow the easy, well-trodden path. Often they glide down that pathway effortlessly before you even notice that you've picked up that bag of crisps rather than an apple. You have to stop them, pull them back and make a conscious effort to go down a different, overgrown, rocky path. It's a more difficult path to follow, but the more you do it, the less overgrown it becomes, and eventually it will be easier and more automatic.

Sometimes your behavioural habits are so ingrained it can be hard to overcome your automatic reflexive behaviours. And, although your neurons are masters in the monumental task of creating new neural pathways, sometimes – especially when tired, stressed or overloaded – they will slip back into their old ways. When you slip into old patterns and munch on those crisps, don't give up or berate yourself. Think about what will help you travel the new path, as the more you travel it, the easier it becomes.

These exercises aim to help you find ways to create new habits and change, and to think about how you manage when you have inevitable setbacks.

Setting meaningful goals

There's plenty of evidence to suggest that goal-setting helps you be clear about what you want to achieve, identify how to achieve this, and means you are more likely to succeed. A goal is an outcome that can be achieved or completed, such as doing something new or developing a more compassionate inner voice. Any of the exercises in this book could be used as goals. However, although goal-setting sounds easy, getting it right is often harder and takes more thought than you might anticipate. So give yourself time, and be patient and kind to yourself. Here are some tips to help you set and stick to your goals:

Make goals specific and measurable. 'I will be more sociable' is not specific; 'I will meet with one friend for a coffee per month' is.

Identify when you will do your goal if possible. 'I will walk home from work on Wednesday', for example.

Start with something you enjoy. You are much more likely to achieve a goal you feel positive about.

Ask yourself how confident you are that you will achieve a goal, from 0–100 per cent. Start with goals that you are above 50 per cent confident you will achieve. Success will likely encourage you and more difficult goals can always be tackled later.

Set value-based goals, as you are more likely to stick to them. If one of your values (see pages 36–41) is 'to be more connected', you might set a goal of phoning one friend every week.

Set positive targets, focusing on what are you moving towards rather away from. 'To stop feeling anxious' is not a positive target; 'to do two things a day that help me relax' is.

Set learning goals rather than achievement goals, as they are more likely to be adhered to. Instead of saying, 'I will eat less cake', you could say, 'I want to discover five healthy snacks to eat.'

Celebrate and reward yourself when you achieve any of your small steps or targets. Positively reinforcing what you have done motivates you to do more.

Watch out for your inner critic sneaking in, and take steps to develop a more compassionate inner voice (see pages 160–5).

Do this with someone else. Research suggests you are much less likely to back out of something you have arranged to do with someone else.

Use the illustration opposite to set what you want to achieve at the top of the goal mountain. Then break this down into smaller steps to help you reach your goal. The more achievable the steps, the better. Regularly monitor your progress to help you decide when you have completed one step and want to move to the next. This will also help you to determine when you might need to re-evaluate your goals, and to identify any barriers you might have to manage. It's important not to be rigid about your goals, as sometimes life gets in the way of achieving them. You might need to think of other ways to meet goals, or redefine goals in line with your values and changes in your life.

Incorporating small habits into your life

Sometimes the things we want to achieve are small things, such as feeling more gratitude, reading a book, going for a short walk or drinking more water. Often these small habits can have a significant impact on your life. Use these four steps to help incorporate them in your life:

1. Link the new behaviour to existing behaviour

Linking into existing habits means your new habits are more likely to be maintained, and the old behaviour creates a stimulus for the new behaviour. Tie gratitude into your existing bedtime routine or when you have your morning coffee. Incorporate going for a walk into your trip to get said coffee, by walking a longer route. Read your book when you are commuting, or drink half a glass of water every time you check your emails.

2. Keep it small, specific and achievable

If you feel successful in doing the task, you are more likely to keep going. Start by reading two pages of your book, or drinking two swigs of water from your bottle. Write down one thing you are grateful for every night. If you feel good completing these small steps, you may even feel like doing more.

3. Introduce one thing at a time

Doing too much at the same time means you are more likely to overwhelm yourself, start to associate negative feelings with the habits and give up.

4. Ensure your environment aids you in completing the task

Leave your gratitude journal and pen beside the bed, or keep your book in your bag, plan your walk route on your phone, or fill a bottle of water to drink during the day, with lines marked on it for how much you will drink before you email.

EXERCISE 3

Responding to (or dealing with) setbacks

Setbacks are normal! If you are tired, stressed or overwhelmed, your brain is much more likely to slip into old habits. Instead of beating yourself up, remind yourself of these key things:

Setbacks are not failures; they can be helpful to learn from. Don't criticize and blame yourself: see if there is anything you can learn to make it easier next time.

Setbacks normally happen at times when you don't have the brain resources to keep going down a new, more difficult path.

Having a setback doesn't mean you are back to square one. Once you've made a start, it will be easier to use that new path again, and you are likely to get back to where you were more quickly.

Keep the focus on your achievements - setbacks don't wipe out them out.

Setbacks are prime fodder for your inner critic, so use the exercises on pages 163-5 if you spot the critic emerging.

Routes off the Stress Roundabout

(engaging your para-sympathetic system + creating feel-good sensations)

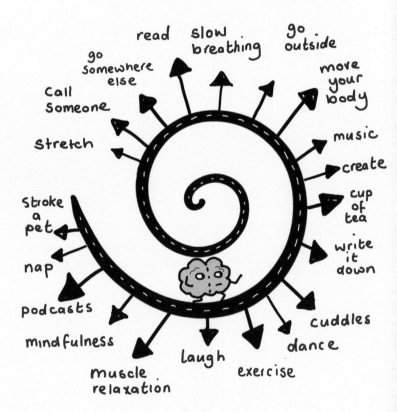

Let's get physical

There's one part of the emotions cycle we haven't focused on yet: physiological feelings in our bodies that both create emotions and are responses to emotions. Firstly, though, I need to introduce you to the sympathetic nervous system's partner-in-crime, the parasympathetic nervous system.

Like Bert and Ernie, or Laurel and Hardy, the sympathetic and parasympathetic nervous systems complement each other, working together to regulate and manage your body and the energy you require. While the sympathetic nervous system prepares you for action, the parasympathetic nervous system generally works to calm your body down and engage in restful activity. A feeling of calm is normally associated with this system being at work. Sometimes called the rest and digest system, the parasympathetic system also has a vital role in regulating your breathing, heart rate and immune response.

This part of the emotions cycle, where emotions interact with physical sensations, can be overlooked. Perhaps because it seems like it doesn't involve higher cognitive functions (although, of course, it does). Yet intervening at a physical level can have an impact on physiological sensations, creating different feelings in your body and potentially creating different emotions. Doing something simple like slowing down your breathing engages your parasympathetic system, which creates feel-good sensations in your body.

Of course, it doesn't change the trigger, so if something in the environment is making you anxious or sad, it may still need to be dealt with. But intervening at a bodily level can calm you down enough to help untangle the jumble in your head, work out what to do, recognize the emotions and take positive action, instead of being driven by the emotions.

There are many things you can do to generate feelings and physical sensations in your brain and body. For example, exercise releases chemicals, which induce different physical sensations and pleasant emotions, as does cuddling people you love, doing something kind or getting outside into open space. While you can't necessarily stop emotions arising, you can create other bodily feelings, both short- and long-term, which, in turn, create different balancing emotions.

Recognizing and intervening with the body's stress response is a powerful tool to manage anxiety and other emotions. When you feel bad, often the things you want to do – like hide away in a corner – make it difficult to do the things that you know create more pleasant sensations in your body. However, you can consciously intervene and promote a powerful physical effect which impacts on your feelings, no matter what you are doing.

Just breathe

When we get anxious, our breathing becomes more rapid and shallow, as we take in more oxygen to prepare our bodies for action. If the additional oxygen isn't used, it creates an imbalance of oxygen and carbon dioxide in our bodies, which can result in other physical symptoms associated with anxiety.

Gently deepening the breath helps rebalance the body, calms the 'flight or fight' response and engages the parasympathetic nervous system. This is a new skill to learn, so it takes time and practice, just like learning an instrument. I would recommend trying it when you are not feeling stressed, as it's far easier to learn when you are feeling calm. While you can use this skill to reduce anxiety when you experience it, doing it regularly through the day can also reduce the build-up of stress.

There are many apps and videos online to help you breathe, but this is a simple technique I use to get started:

Sit or stand, then place a hand on your chest and the other hand on your belly. You are trying to breathe into your lower lungs and belly rather than your upper lungs. When you breathe you want to feel your belly rising, with your chest as still as possible.

Try to relax your muscles as much as possible. A good way to do this is to clench your whole body and then release.

Notice a few breaths. Observe how you are breathing right now.

Now gently breathe in through your nose for three slow counts.

Don't force the breath; keep it gentle. Focus on the feeling of the breath coming in through your nose as you count.

Breathe out gently through your mouth for four slow counts.

Keep doing this for a few breaths, or a few minutes if you can.

Adjust the timings to suit. Keeping the in-breath slightly shorter than the out-breath is thought to rebalance the mix of gasses. If you start to feel light-headed or panicky, stop, as you may be forcing your breath too much.

EXERCISE 2

Create feel-good sensations

There are alternative ways to either engage your parasympathetic system or to create other feel-good chemicals in your body, which can be helpful to use when you start feeling stressed. We have already spoken about lots of these in this book: sleep, exercise and a healthy diet work physically on your body and are the building blocks of a healthy mind.

You can also react in the moment to shift how your body is responding. Exercise and movement help release chemicals that give you a boost; they can also help use up that extra oxygen when anxious. Being outside, preferably in green open space and natural light has been shown to decrease stress. Physical touch, cuddles, stroking a pet and massage (if you like them) can create pleasant physical sensations and reduce the stress response. Changing your context, i.e. moving into a different room or environment, can also have this effect. Stretching, yoga, dancing, moving, star jumps or even skipping around your kitchen can create physical responses that disrupt the stress response. Creating and reading are stress-busters for many people too. There are so many ways to intervene with your body stress response and calm things down or create feel-good sensations (I find doodling engages my body relaxation systems). These can be used to disrupt your stress cycle short-term, and build up your resilience longer-term. A few ideas are included in the illustration at the start of this topic on page 140, and I'm sure you can think of lots of your own to add into your toolkit.

EXERCISE 3

Slow down, break and rest

In cultures where busyness is glorified, it is almost a rebellious act to slow down, stop, take breaks and rest. But these are requirements to look after your body and mind, and create a healthy body balance – how you direct and use your energy. Breaks and rest provide time for your body and mind to regulate. They create space in your brain (often the space where ideas come from) and help reduce how much is in your capacity cup.

Yet in writing these sentences, I realize the irony of not following my own advice in taking enough breaks. There are barriers to us taking breaks. They are not the accepted norm at work, and we think they will make us less productive. We feel that we should be busy and doing it all. We feel guilty for taking breaks; we feel they are a luxury. If we don't feel stressed, we feel we are not working hard enough!

Yet all the evidence points to the contrary. Slowing down and resting are necessities for mind and body. Taking breaks makes us more productive (and increases creativity). Even small breaks, such as a walk around the block in between tasks, can have beneficial effects. They help the body heal and recover, they help the brain work better. These gaps in our time, where we stop, rest and recuperate, are inherently good for us.

Use the questions opposite to identify where you can slow down and introduce rest periods into both your work and at home. Downtime and breaks should be held in high regard and considered sacred, worth fighting for and protected at all costs. And now I'm off to take a break from writing this book…

How can I introduce rest periods/breaks?

At home: _____

At work: _____

When would be best to do this?

At home: _____

At work: _____

What will I do during my rest period to ensure it helps my body and brain relax?

At home: _____

At work: _____

What are the barriers to doing this?

At home: _____

At work: _____

How will I make sure the breaks happen?

At home: _____

At work: _____

I'm far more powerful than you think - push me away and i'll pop back stronger!
you're nothing but a pattern of electrical impulses - I'm just going to ignore you

Chapter 6

Responding to Emotions – What We Think

There are many songs about the power of love, but I think we should have more songs about the power of thought, because these fleeting ideas and opinions that pass through our minds have a powerful effect. In this chapter we'll find out that thinking can have the same effect as real-life experiences, that thoughts link with our bodies to create physiological responses, and that the thoughts we have about ourselves are fundamental to how we interact with the world. Thoughts, particularly long-held ones created by well-worn neural pathways in our brains, can appear so automatic, inevitable and factual that they can seem out of our control. However, once we become aware of what our thoughts are telling us and how they impact on us, we can spot the unhelpful stories we tell ourselves and rethink them. We can rewrite our narrative, from a different angle, and create a new chapter going forward. Ultimately, we can learn to engage with our thoughts, and develop patterns of thinking that are beneficial to us and help us look after our mental health. This chapter focuses on harnessing the power of your thoughts to benefit your mind.

The power of thoughts

Thoughts are the running commentary, in verbal or visual form, in our heads. They are also our imagination, self-talk, visualizations, reminders and memories. They are created by our brains and appear to be constantly with us. Sometimes they shout loudly, but at other times our patterns of thoughts are so automatic we don't even notice them. These brain patterns create as much emotion and physiological reaction, and guide our behaviours as much as what is going on in the world around us.

If you don't believe me, imagine picking up a lemon and sucking on it – most people who do this start to salivate and feel the same sensation they would if they actually sucked on a lemon. So, thoughts create real responses. They also shape how we perceive our environment. If we are concerned about something, our attention will be drawn to it, so we are more likely to see it: if you hate dogs, you'll see dogs everywhere. As patterns of thoughts are developed through our past experiences, we anticipate that an event will be scary, and as a result our body gets ready to respond to what we *think* will happen. That's why one person's neutral event can be terrifying for another, because what we think about or predict about an event is much more powerful in creating our response than the event itself. It's all very well saying there's nothing to be scared of, but our mind is telling us there *is* something to be scared of. Our own thoughts can in themselves feel threatening and frightening. Sometimes we just want to get rid of these silly thoughts and push them away, but, much like emotions, the more we suppress them, the more likely they are to pop up with greater force.

Our thoughts also tell us stories about ourselves and other people that can guide our actions. We tell ourselves that we won't be able to cope, that people don't like us, or that we are a certain type of person. While our stories are just constructs, we believe them, and can become so tied into them that they define us. We may begin to operate only within the confines of our stories, never venturing beyond. Although many of these stories are based on out-of-date or incorrect information, such as childhood experiences or the narratives we have received in our lives from society, our belief in them means we confirm them by what we see and what we do. We see the stories as truths, when they are only perceptions; a construction, rather than a reflection of reality.

Our trains of thought are perpetually journeying through our minds; we have so many thoughts during a day. We need lots of these trains to guide our behaviour, to help keep us on track and to remember where we have been before. Some thoughts are unhelpful to us, some are just random brain connections firing together – meaningless by-products. Some are created by natural brain biases; others are long-held patterns of thoughts developed through life. And the thoughts that stand out most are the ones that shout the loudest or have been there the longest. Long-held patterns of thoughts will be supported by well-used neural networks in your brain, and so their trains glide around your mind with ease. They've been there so long they feel inevitable and like reality. The thoughts we notice most are often the scary or unpleasant ones, which demand our attention by creating sensations in our bodies that make them hard to ignore. This means the thoughts in the quiet coaches are often overlooked, as the loud ones drown them out.

Those perpetually running trains of thought have a huge amount of power over what we see, feel and do. This is a reciprocal relationship, because how we feel affects our thoughts. When we are down, our thoughts tend to be consistent with our mood, so we are more likely to focus on the negatives. We believe our brains because it feels true, but it's not, as this information is filtered and distorted by focus, bias, past experiences and beliefs. The wonderful thing is we can decide not to go along with certain narratives, and we can guide our thoughts to be more beneficial to us. By becoming aware of the stories our thoughts are telling us, and stepping back from them, we can learn to respond helpfully to our thoughts.

Spotting thoughts

To be able to respond to your thoughts, you first need to spot them. This isn't always easy, as the trains of thought can be so fast and automatic we don't always notice them. We've already spoken about spotting your thoughts a few times in the book – remember those judgements we stood in the spotlight when shaming our emotions (see pages 82-3), the comparisons we make (see pages 106-13), or those attributions when we experience imposter syndrome (see pages 120-1)? All those are thoughts you have noticed. Now it's time to start spotting other thoughts that may be impacting on your emotions. Thoughts can both create emotions and result from emotions – a two-way path. The first steps are to notice the thoughts you might be having that are unhelpful to you:

Spot those thoughts. Pause and see if you can observe what is going through your mind. Ask yourself, 'What am I thinking now?' What is it you are focusing on? It can be helpful to do this when you are feeling bad, so you can identify patterns of thought that contribute to these feelings.

Think about how helpful these thoughts are. Recognize these are thoughts, not facts. How helpful are these thoughts to you right now? Notice how the thoughts are making you feel. Do they impact on your actions? You can use the emotions cycle (see pages 72-7) to work out how they impacted on what you did and how you felt.

Recognizing patterns of thoughts

Often, thoughts follow common themes and patterns, so understanding these patterns can help you spot them. Here are some common patterns of thought. Tick off the ones you experience, as this can help you spot them when they happen.

Blaming yourself – when you internalize and take responsibility for things that are really not your fault (or at least not as much as you think they are).

The not-so-magnificent mind-readers – we make assumptions about what people think of us. Turns out we are not the great fortune-tellers we think we are, and we are often wrong. While people may pass judgement, often they are too caught up in their own thoughts to think about us.

Jumping to conclusions – when you race ahead and fill uncertainty with inaccurate certainty, predicting the future: 'I will make a mess of this presentation.'

The belief-consistent brain-filter – your brain filters information quickly, which means it's much more likely to see information that fits with what it already knows. If you believe you are rubbish at something, your brain will select information consistent with this. If you are scared of something, you will start to see examples of this everywhere. Your brain is filtering information to see what you expect to see, which means you fail to notice inconsistencies that might tell another story.

Mass assumption – when you draw conclusions based on small details. This often happens with mistakes: you did badly on an essay, so clearly you are rubbish. You got some feedback to change a work assignment, so you can't do your job properly. Someone made a negative comment about you, obviously everybody thinks this. When you take a step back these assumptions look wildly inaccurate, but in the moment they seem accurate and affect how we feel.

Being stuck in your black-and-white story – we can have strong views of what we are like or what other people are like, to the extent that we define ourselves by this; but people's personalities are not stagnant. Seeing and defining ourselves narrowly in this way can place unhelpful limits on ourselves and what we do. The classic example I see is when people define themselves as 'not someone who gets stressed or experiences mental health concerns'. This means they fail to see when they are affected by stress until they reach a point of overwhelm, when it can't be disregarded anymore. Allowing ourselves to see shades of grey in who we are and how the world operates can be uncomfortable at first, but reaps long-term rewards.

EXERCISE 3

Responding to your thoughts

Once you have spotted thoughts that are having an unhelpful impact on how you are feeling, there are two main ways that you can respond: by stepping back, choosing to observe them and deciding which ones to engage with, or by interacting with them directly and challenging them as an objective observer. Both approaches work in similar ways, by enabling you to view your thoughts from a distance, rather than being caught up in them and find your behaviour driven by them. In my work, I've noticed that different people find these two techniques helpful, so try them out and see which works for you, or pop them both in your toolkit and use them interchangeably when they work best.

Deciding which thoughts to engage with

It is possible to stand back, notice your thoughts, recognize you don't have to be pulled along on this ride and actively decide which train to get on. You can observe these trains of thought approaching, 'Oh look, there's my brain telling me that again', give them a little nod to say hello and then let them pass by, safe in the knowledge that you don't have to jump on board if you don't want to. Just because we have a thought (and there are so many reasons we can have thoughts), we don't need to take them seriously and believe them. Follow these five steps to help you decide which thought train to board:

1. Step back and observe your thoughts, so that you see them for what they are: simply thoughts that don't have to guide your behaviour. Instead of just having the thought, telling yourself 'I notice I am having a thought that…' can help you step back from it. Remind yourself: thoughts are not facts. They may feel real, but that doesn't mean they are true; although they feel scary, these thoughts are just thoughts.

2. Acknowledge it. Say to yourself, 'Hello, thought train, I see what you are telling me and that's okay. I'm going to watch you pass through my mind. I don't need to get on board and believe you. I can learn to notice you pass instead.'

3. Recognize stories and patterns. If you notice common patterns that your thoughts follow (Exercise 2 can help with this), you can identify the story the train is telling. For example, 'Here's the story train telling me that I have no friends.' Remind yourself it's just a story passing through your brain, and let it pass.

4. Accept it, don't fight it. Your brain is doing its best to help you out, although it's not always successful, so instead of fighting against it, you can give it a nod of acknowledgement. Tell it, 'Thank you, for that thought. I see you are trying to help me', and then let it pass, rather than being directly influenced by it.

5. See your thoughts in a different light. One technique, which can seem a bit silly but allows you to relate to your thoughts differently, is to sing them to yourself or say them in a silly voice when you notice them. This seems to help people stand back from their thoughts and see them as something they don't have to take seriously. (One person I worked with thoroughly enjoyed singing them out in a thrash-metal style, which made it very difficult for them to take their thoughts seriously.)

Challenging your thoughts
This is not about creating positive thinking, but rather looking at your thoughts more objectively and questioning their validity. It's about prompting your mind to be fair and open. If you try to disagree too vehemently with your thoughts or push them away, they may fight back stronger, but you can work with your

thoughts to help get a different perspective. Ultimately, you want to increase the flexibility of your thoughts and shift from black-and-white thinking to a wider, fairer, finer-grained perspective. Use the following three steps to help with this approach:

1. Stand back and look at what your thoughts are saying. Write them down.

2. Now ask yourself the following questions:

Is this a fair assessment of the situation?

What meaning am I drawing from this situation?

Are there factors influencing how I see this situation right now? For example, high stress levels, lack of sleep or high emotions?

What's the bigger picture?

Will this matter in a month or a year's time?

What would I say to a friend in this situation?

Has my brain fallen into any of the thinking patterns from Exercise 2 or the opening illustration on page 150?

Is there any evidence to support other conclusions?

Are there any other ways to think about this?

3. What conclusion have you come to? What is a more realistic and balanced way to look at this situation? Write it down. Remind yourself of this when you notice this pattern of thinking again.

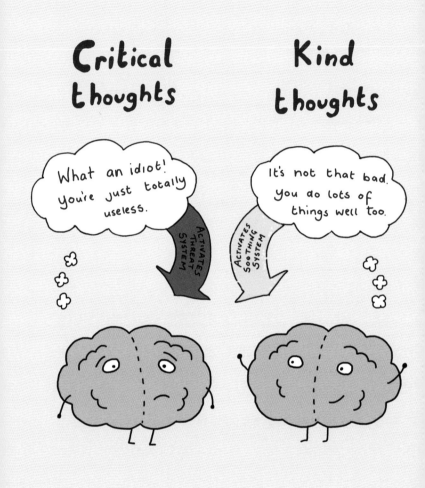

Inner critic

What would you think if you heard someone saying these things to one of your friends? I'm guessing you'd think they were a bully, and downright rude and nasty. You might even march up to this person and tell them they were out of order. You'd most likely tell your friend that this person was factually incorrect and boost them up, providing all the evidence you can think of to prove this bully was wrong.

Yet this bully often exists in our own heads. It is there to berate us, perhaps repeating comments we heard at some point in our lives, tapping into our self-doubt, or spotting our vulnerabilities and digging away at them. Instead of outing this critic for the persecutor that it is, we believe it without question. We take the words on board without doubting the accuracy of them and accept their conclusion as correct, without objectively considering the evidence.

We fail to apply the same boundaries to the bully in our heads that we would to the real-life bully. While we stand back and objectively state it is unacceptable when it happens to a friend, we are far more subjective with ourselves. As a result, this inner bully gets off far too lightly and is allowed to shout nasty comments to us as we go about our daily business. We can become so used to this background nastiness it becomes insidious, sneaking around and subtly undermining us to the point we don't even notice it.

We all have an inner dialogue running through our heads, and what this says to us affects how we react, our brain chemistry and how we feel. Imagine someone shouting nasty and critical comments at you all day. How would you feel? You might feel deflated, sad, anxious, demotivated or overwhelmed. This inner critic triggers a threat response, making us anxious and tense. Nobody deserves a constant barrage of criticism, especially when it is directed at them from their own brain. So it's time to turn this around and start working on being your inner best friend instead.

Outing your bully

The first step in dealing with your inner critic is spotting it. Bullies
need to be called out for what they are, and this one tends to
be a compulsive liar that feeds on self-doubt and vulnerabilities.
By noticing your inner critic, you can bring it out of the shadows
and give it a serious talking to. Exposing it starts to take away its
power, because you can start to look at it with more objectivity
and apply the same scrutiny to it that you would to someone
else's bully.

**The best way to out your bully is to notice when it is at work and
what it is telling you.** A clue that your bully is at work is that you
are feeling bad. Common fodder for your bully is making a
mistake, thinking you have done something wrong or feeling silly
or embarrassed about something. Sometimes there might be a
clear trigger that sets off your critic, but at other times it may pick
on the most innocuous of events, which is much harder to spot.

**When you notice the signs that your inner critic is at work ask
yourself, what is it telling you?** Write it down. Is it calling you
stupid? Not as able to do things as well as other people? There
tends to be patterns in what it says, so you may find your bully
repeating itself frequently.

Try to imagine what your inner critic looks like. This will help to
externalize it from your own brain. Is it a nasty troll telling you
that you are no good? Or a malevolent fox, sneaking around,
dropping hints at your incompetence? Visualizing your inner critic

may help you to view it more objectively. The aim is to notice it and the criticisms it is throwing at you.

Use more objectivity

Now you've outed your bullying inner critic, it's time to cast some real scrutiny over what it is telling you. To do this, we are going to use the concept illustrated at the start of this topic on page 160; that we are much more objective with other people than we are with ourselves. It is difficult to be an objective bystander to your own circumstance. Your bully is intrinsically tied in with past experience, beliefs and emotions, and therefore it can be hard to separate your bully from how you feel. We are much more able to cast a critical and objective eye over someone else's situation and bully. We also tend to be more compassionate to other people compared with ourselves.

Imagine speaking to a friend who is in the same situation that you were in when your bully kicked off. What would you say to them? Would you tell them they were stupid for making a mistake? Or would you be more compassionate? My guess is the latter, as we tend to look at someone else's situation more objectively than our own. So, we can be confident that this is a fairer thing to say to someone in this situation than what we, or our inner critic, say to ourselves.

Develop a more compassionate voice

So, we've noticed that our inner critic is unfairly harsh, and that when we look at the situation more objectively we tend to view it more kindly. The next step is to develop a more compassionate inner voice. When we treat ourselves kindly, we trigger our soothing system, which makes us feel safe, relaxed and cared for. This in turn makes us feel more in control of a difficult situation.

Think about what you would say to a friend in the same situation. How would you make them feel better? How would you question the critical bully speaking to them? How would you look at the situation in a more balanced way? Now apply this more objective voice to yourself. This new compassionate voice is your inner nurturer, who is there to look after you.

This may feel artificial at first, and you may not believe what you are telling yourself. It takes a while to break down and rebuild patterns of thinking. The inner critic has a well-worn path that it can travel along smoothly, while your new inner nurturer must battle through an infrequently used and overgrown path. Yet the more we encourage our inner nurturer, the more easily it travels along this path, while the path of the inner critic becomes more tangled and overgrown, so it finds it harder to reach us.

You are more likely to slip back into old patterns when you are feeling down. When your inner bully sneaks back in, it means you need more nurturing. Instead of berating yourself for going back to your old ways, see it as a sign to be even kinder to yourself.

Introducing the 'shoulds'

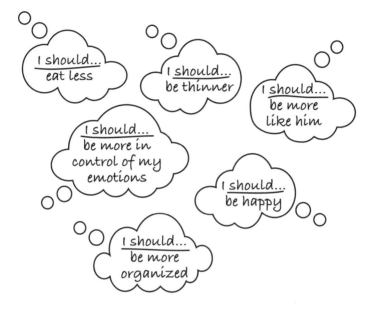

I'd like to introduce you to the 'shoulds'. I picture them as cute little creatures in the shape of thought bubbles, who draw you in with their big eyes and trick you into thinking they are doing you a favour by setting you motivating goals. They tell you what you *should* be doing, what kind of person you *should* be, what kind of parent you *should* be, how you *should* be feeling. They seem reasonable creatures, as why wouldn't we want to better ourselves? However, the 'shoulds' latch onto inaccuracies and misperceptions, and feed on self-doubt, comparisons, unrealistic expectations and self-criticism to create large gaps between who we are and who we think we should be. They inhabit the space between expectation and reality, and as a result take up far too much space in our brains.

The 'shoulds' whisper that you should be happy/be able to do this/feel undying love for your child all the time/be capable of 'doing it all'. By telling us what we *should* be, they have a nasty habit of implying what we *shouldn't* be. They might never explicitly say it, but it's what they really mean. You *shouldn't* be feeling anxious/find raising children hard/struggle to juggle work with children/find being a stay-at-home mum/dad difficult. Basically, they are telling you that you are not doing well enough. The 'shoulds' also like to pull our children in with us. They tell us that our children *should* be reading/behaving better/be out of nappies.

'Shoulds' are not daft: they know that whenever we believe them a gap opens up between reality and where we should be. This gap is where the 'shoulds' reside: a land of inevitable disappointment and shame at falling short of unattainable achievements and unrealistic expectations. They make you believe that if only you could get to 'the other side', life would be better, you'd be happier and all would be well with the world. The promise of 'the other side' is a false one. The 'shoulds' trick you into thinking that you need to change drastically before you can achieve your goals and feel good, when actually nearly everything you need is already in your grasp. They create a breeding pit for emotions of shame, guilt and disappointment, where they thrive. And they're hidden so well that instead of pointing the finger of blame at the 'shoulds' (the thoughts that create these feelings) we place the responsibility on ourselves. So, mind those 'should gaps' and notice when you fall into them.

We do need to spot the worthwhile 'shoulds', however, because sometimes they can have great potential, and have even been known to change the world. When Caroline Criado-Perez said there should be more women statues in Parliament Square, this aligned with her values, and started a campaign which made this happen. When Greta Thunberg said we should take more care of the environment, she used this should to motivate her into action. These women converted their 'shoulds' into direct actions; not what they *should* do, but what they *can* do. Recognizing the difference between a 'should' worth fighting for and one that is self-criticism means we can convert the former into actionable and tangible goals, and learn to ignore the inward-looking, guilt-inducing 'shoulds'.

Spotting your 'shoulds'

Use the opening illustration on page 166 as a prompt to identify your own 'shoulds'. What are they telling you? List them out on a fresh piece of paper.

Closing the 'should' gap

Work out which 'shoulds' are worth holding on to. Which ones make you feel bad? Are the 'shoulds' telling you that life would be so much better if you got to the other side of the 'should' gap? Who says you should? Are these voices from the past? Is it something you believe in or something you've been told you should do by other people or society?

Try to separate your 'shoulds' into these four categories:

1. Should sticks – used to beat yourself up unfairly.

2. Should myths – tell you that life would be better if you got to the other side.

3. Should wishes – you wish these were the case, but are they unrealistic goals or worth expending energy on?

4. Should values – these are consistent with your values and can help direct where you are going.

For the first two categories it can be helpful to refer back to some of the techniques from earlier in the book: see The Power of Thoughts on pages 150–9. For the third category, recognize that this is a wish, but it doesn't mean you should be doing it. If it is not realistic, try to actively decide how much you want to engage with the thought (see Responding to Your Thoughts exercise on pages 156–9). Or you may want to challenge your idea of what would really happen if this 'should' did occur. For example, are you telling yourself life would be better if you lost weight? Ask yourself if this is really the case.

EXERCISE 3

Transforming the 'should' to 'can'

There is only a small number of 'shoulds' that are worth listening to and that you want to hold on to. This final category of 'Should values' need to be shifted from intangible 'shoulds' into tangible 'cans', which allow them to be converted into actionable goals instead (see Change and Goals, pages 132–9). For example, if you think you should do more for the environment, then you can convert this from a guilt-inducing 'should' into an achievable and tangible action by saying, 'I can try to use reusable packaging.' Relist your 'shoulds' that are worth listening to and convert them to 'cans':

I should…   **I can…**

Cat-ostrophizing

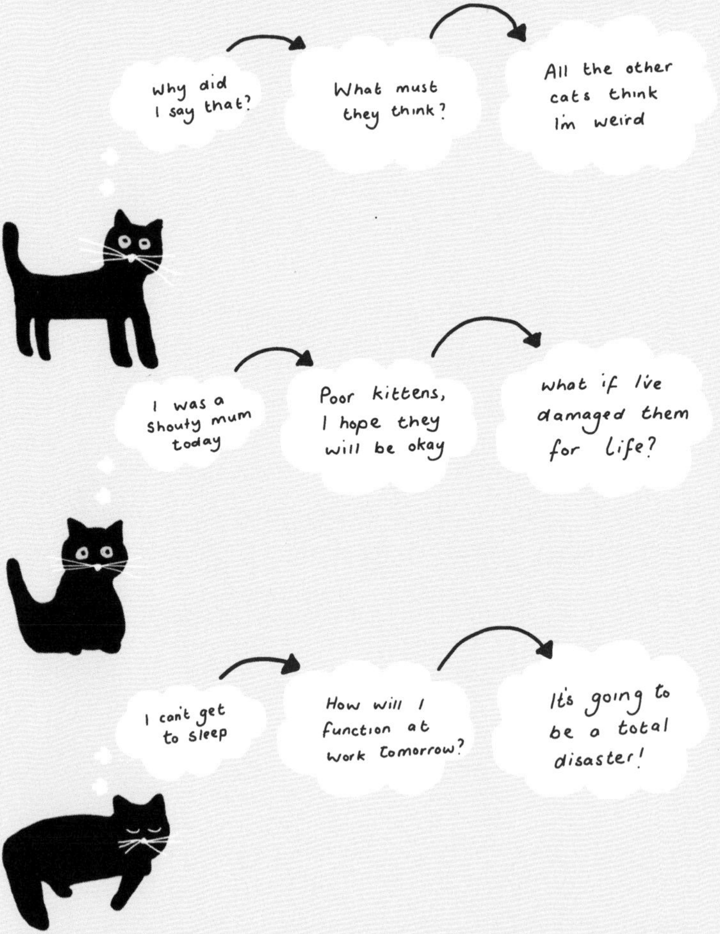

Catastrophe alert!

Your brain is not only an impressive threat detector, predicting where you need to direct your attention and energy, but also a fantastic future-planning and anticipating organ. Combining these impressive abilities can be hugely helpful in directing behaviour towards goals. But, you'll have guessed by now that as helpful as many of our brain's abilities are, there is often a downside to these skills.

Sometimes we combine these predictive powers and threat detectors into an explosive combination where our brains notice what they perceive as a negative event, and jump too far ahead, predicting too much threat. Before we know it, our brains have run away with themselves and we are facing a catastrophe of supernova proportions, where threats abound everywhere and we have convinced ourselves the worst-case scenario is bound to happen. It's obviously going to be a disaster of epic proportions!

Psychologists use a term to describe this: 'catastrophizing'. It all starts with a tiny insignificant event…a toddler tantrum, a burnt meal, a minor slip-up, something tactless we said to our friend. Or perhaps something bigger – a lower grade in an exam than expected, a day of shouting too much at the kids, some unpleasant physical symptoms. If it was your friend in this situation you would tell them 'it's no big deal', or 'let's think about this sensibly', but, for whatever reason, your brain does not behave like a friend. It notices this information, ponders it and, before you know it, the starter gun has sounded and it's off, faster than Usain Bolt, to the disastrous chasm of a finish line where Armageddon seems inevitable. You haven't just got a grade C in the exam – you've ruined your life forever. It wasn't just a shouty day (that we all have) – you've damaged your kids for life. You didn't just say something a bit silly – none of your friends will ever want speak to you again. It's a full-blown catastrophe.

It may seem ridiculous out of context. But in the middle of it all, when emotions are high, it's not only difficult to rein in your thoughts – these outlandish conclusions feel inevitable and true. Of course they will happen, there's no doubt in your mind. And that sets your mind rocketing even further into the explosive catastrophic chasm of doom. While hurtling down the chasm, your mind makes a further prediction: while it vastly overestimates the chances of full-scale disaster, conversely it also vastly underestimates how you will cope in the very slim chance the worst does happen. Most of us think we will crumble when bad things happen, but actually very few people do and most cope far better than they anticipate.

Certain situations lend themselves particularly well to taking the leap into the chasm of catastrophe. It's probably no surprise that we are more likely to do this when our capacity cup is bubbling over (see pages 44–51), as we don't have the brain space to sit back and consider the situation from a distance. Uncertainty also provides the perfect starting block for your thoughts to run off with themselves. Humans tend to like certainty, and we find it comforting to plan the future, which creates more certainty. So when there is uncertainty in our lives, this can cause anxiety, and our brains can try to create certainty by filling in the blanks, often predicting the worst-case scenario with an unhelpful pseudo-certainty, which backfires and makes us feel worse.

These exercises are designed to put some hurdles in place to stop your mind sprinting to the chasm of catastrophe and slow it down on its way.

Putting up hurdles

When you become more in tune with your thoughts (as I hope you now are), you may notice that the starter's gun has fired and your thoughts are off. Stop. As soon as you've noticed the race has started, you've already busted your thoughts and their pace starts to slow. Now it's time to put some more hurdles in their way to slow them down further, make them take another route, or perhaps even go back to the start line. Ask yourself these questions:

How likely is it that your brain's worst-case scenario is actually going to happen?

What are the facts and stats around this?

If this does happen, what can you do?

What's most likely to happen?

Is the worst-case scenario truly a disaster, or would you survive it?

Write down your answers to these questions. Your thoughts tend to run in patterns, so this race will most likely happen again, and when it does you can remind yourself of your answers, so that hopefully you won't be dragged into the race to a catastrophic ending again.

Gratitude: zooming in on the here and now

As a typical Scottish person with high inbuilt levels of cynicism, when I first heard about 'gratitude' I was hugely sceptical. It all sounded a little contrived and simplistic. However, apart from there being robust research to back it up, it makes sense when you think about it. Gratitude works by shifting your mind's attention from its automatic negative bias to see the wider picture – what you have now that you are grateful for and what makes you feel good. Shifting your focus to this means you are more likely to not only notice the wider picture more in the future, but also remember it. In the short term it's not going to override your brain's tendency to over-imagine risk and race off into the future, but it is creating longer-term patterns of thoughts that will slow the race, or stop it happening all together. The more regularly you do this, and the more you notice and are grateful for small things, the more beneficial it can be.

The simplest way to do this is to regularly stop and write down three things for which you are grateful. They don't have to be big, in fact, the smaller, the better. By writing these down, you are more likely to consolidate them in your memory. You are creating a gratitude trace in your brain. Lots of people like to do this before bed, and from a brain point of view that's sensible, as sleep helps memories consolidate, so you may be more likely to create these gratitude links in your brain at this time.

Tolerating uncertainty

Uncertainty can make your thoughts start to race, but you can help yourself tolerate it. These techniques are also useful for another psychology word I love – rumination – which is when we get stuck on worries we can't necessarily find solutions for (often because there aren't any). It can be helpful to think about what is and what isn't in your control. You can't change what is out of your control, so your resources are best directed to responding to what *is* in your control. Use the illustration as a prompt to identify and categorize your worries. Put those that are in your control in the blue balloons and those that aren't in the pink balloons.

For worries that are out of your control:

Recognize and validate your emotions around them. Try to recognize your thinking around them. Use the thought strategies on pages 154–9 to help decide how best to respond.

Shift your attention back to the present – focus on your breathing.

Try to find ways to let these worries go – talk them through with a friend or do something that relaxes you.

For worries that are in your control:

Untangle what is making you feel stressed – you can use the brain tangle exercise on page 56 to help.

Think about how you can manage these stressors – use the problem-solving exercise on pages 98–9 for ideas to help.

Think about helpful next steps you can take.

· untangle thoughts
· write them down
· problem solve
· plan next steps
Holding on to what I can Control
letting go of what I can't
· Validate emotions
· identify + respond to thoughts
· Find ways to set aside

Putting It All Together

By now I hope you have used this book to build your own personalized toolkit to look after your mind. The contents of your toolkit are unique to you, and will enable you to place looking after your mind at the centre of your life, and give it the attention it deserves.

I couldn't possibly fit all of the existing psychological techniques or evidence-based tools into this book, so add to your toolkit as you find more tools that are useful to you. Sometimes what works well for you at one point may not work so well at other times, so it's also important to be flexible in adapting your toolkit when necessary.

While having a toolkit will help you look after your mind proactively, no one is immune to dips in their mental health. Even people who know all the theory and techniques in the world – clinical psychologists, for example – are not immune to problems. Mental health and experiencing distress is a human condition, and, given the right (or rather wrong) circumstances, anyone's mental health can suffer.

It's important to recognize the signs that your mental health is deteriorating, so you can take positive action. Denying that it is suffering is not stoic, it's just more likely to extend your distress and may exacerbate things. But that doesn't make it easy: deteriorations in mental health can be insidious and gradual, and the symptoms themselves can make it difficult to recognize or to seek help. We can feel like an imposter: 'I don't deserve help as there's nothing in my life to feel bad about'. We tell ourselves, 'I'm not a depressed/anxious/stressed person', but this negates the fact that *all* humans can experience these feelings.

There can also be multiple barriers to seeking help. You may be worried you will be dismissed or invalidated. You may think you are somehow weird or different. Having seen many people who have experienced difficulties with their mental health, I can reassure you that your experience will be shared, because we have far more in common than separates us and that includes our experiences of distress. You may think you don't deserve help. There's also no denying that the thought of opening up to people can be horribly scary, particularly if this is to a healthcare provider you have never met before. However, a range of evidence-based treatments exist for mental health difficulties and in seeking help for this you should be taken just as seriously as if you had physical health symptoms.

The illustration on the next page is designed to help you identify what being mentally healthy means to you, the signs that your mental health is suffering, and the steps and actions you can take when you notice this. Some of these

Being Mentally Healthy for me is:

Signs that my mental health is suffering:

What helps me when this happens:

Signs I may need extra help:

steps may be about seeking professional help when necessary. It may also be worth looking in advance at the provisions available in your area, or how you would access help if required, as healthcare systems can be difficult to navigate, even more so if you are stressed, distressed or overwhelmed. Having knowledge can be empowering in itself, so that you feel that there are options available to you.

Mental health first-aid kit

We all have a physical health first-aid kit in our homes, and I would love for there to be a time when our mental health concerns have parity. We can start by putting together a first-aid kit for our minds, for times when we notice that our mental health is starting to deteriorate. It is much easier to have this prepared beforehand, because some of the characteristics of distress are that the mind feels jumbled, we just don't know where to start and making decisions can be difficult. Having a kit to hand reduces the energy and effort we have to exert in planning what actions to take.

Your mental health first-aid kit might include information on helplines to text or call and how to access direct help in your local area. Seeking professional help is not a failure – to me it is as normal as seeking help when you have an infection or broken bone. If you are experiencing low mood, anxiety, or any form of distress or emotion that is impacting detrimentally on your wellbeing or functioning, and/or has lasted for more than two weeks, it is worth speaking to a healthcare provider to determine whether treatment would be beneficial to you. Certain physical medical conditions can also induce feelings we label as anxiety or depression, and it's always worth getting them checked out too.

I recently asked a range of people what they would put in a mental health first-aid kit, and the illustration opposite shows some of the themes that emerged. Use this to think about what you would put in your own kit. Write them down as prompts and keep them to hand.

Some caveats before we finish

It's important to acknowledge that sometimes when we are distressed, it is a normal reaction to an abnormal set of circumstances. For example, most people are distressed when a loved one dies. This is completely understandable; distress can be a typical human response to stressful situations. However, it can be difficult sometimes to work out whether your distress is a natural response to circumstances or if you are experiencing difficulties with your mental health that could benefit from help. Don't be scared to ask for help – talking it through can provide context, help you normalize how you are feeling and put steps in place to remedy it.

Some of the strongest predictors of mental health difficulties are real-life circumstances – including financial difficulties,

My Mental Health First Aid Kit
photos of good times - to remind me I will feel good again
Sources of support - websites, phone numbers
a pen + notebook to write it all down
Items that help me relax and feel good e.g. blanket, breathing apps, book
Reminders of supportive statements from family, friends + past me.
permission to give myself a break prompts e.g. take a walk, go outside
feel good playlist
A list of strategies to help when I feel bad
helpful mantras + statements

dealing with bullying, undermining and abusive relationships (at work or at home) or living through traumatic events. In these situations you are experiencing something that is creating chronic stress and impacting on your mental health. You have something in your life that is creating distress because it is distressing.

While for most people the techniques in this book should help, if you are in these circumstances treatment is best targeted at removing the stressor from your life, if you can. If someone is being bullied, as a psychologist I don't just want to help them cope with this; instead I want to deal directly with the stressor creating the distress, and therefore deal directly with the bullying. Of course, on an individual level targeting issues like your financial situation, bullying at work or an abusive relationship can be extremely difficult. So, while you might find some of the techniques in this book helpful, the priority in these situations should be direct action at changing your circumstances, with help, if required.

On a societal level, individual treatment of mental health difficulties is not the full story when it comes to mental health, it's just part of the solution. We also need societal measures to target the factors – including poverty, trauma and prolonged chronic stress – that, through research, we know have the greatest impact on mental health.

Some last words

I hope you've come to the end of this book armed with a toolkit to help with your mental health in busy modern life, and feel confident looking after your mind. I also hope you've arrived at the end of the book with the belief that we all have mental health that needs looking after, and that distress is not necessarily abnormal, it's part of being human. Going forward with this belief will be helpful not only to yourself, as you will be more open to thinking about your own emotions, noticing them, taking action and seeking help when required, but also for us all going forward as a society. It will help shift attitudes from the concept that mental health is something that just some people have, and which we respond to only when it goes wrong, to the idea that it's something we all have that requires looking after proactively on an individual, collective and societal level. Recognizing that our minds are impacted on by our whole lives, and that mental health is inseparable from our physical health and environment, puts us in a strong position. It allows us to reduce stigma, increase our knowledge and look after our mental health in an informed, evidence-based way. I hope this book has played a part in opening up the discussion.

Further Reading

You can find out a little more about some of the topics discussed in this book with these further resources.

Introduction
For understanding more on mental health myths:

Austin, Jehannine & Landrum Peay, Holly, *How to Talk with Families About Genetics and Psychiatric Illness*, W. W. Norton & Company, 2011

Filer, Nathan, *This Book will Change your Mind about Mental Health*, Faber & Faber, 2019

For more information on the workings of the brain:
Burnett, Dean, *The Idiot Brain*, Guardian Faber Publishing, 2017

New Scientist, *The Brain: A User's Guide*, Hodder & Stoughton Ltd, 2018

For more on how the mind and body are linked:
Macciochi, Jenna, Dr., Chapter 5: 'Mental health matters' in *Immunity: the Science of Staying Well*, Harper Non Fiction, 2020

Marchant, Jo, Cure: *A journey into the Science of Mind over Body*, Canongate Books, 2017

Don't forget the basics
Hammond, Claudia, *The Art of Rest: How to Find Respite in the Modern Age*, Canongate Books, 2019

Hardy, Jane, *365 Days of Self-Care: A Journal*, Orion Spring, 2018

Reading, Suzy, *The Self-Care Revolution: Smart Habits & Simple Practices to Allow You to Flourish*, Aster, 2017

Seal, Clare, *Real Life Money: An Honest Guide to Taking Control of Your Finances*, Headline Home, 2020

Walker, Matthew, *Why We Sleep: The New Science of Sleep and Dreams*, Penguin, 2018

The five pillars
Kabat- Zinn, Jon, *Wherever You Go, There You Are: Mindfulness Meditation for Everyday Life*, Piatkus, 2004

Values
Harris, Russ, *The Happiness Trap: Stop Struggling, Start Living*, Robinson Publishing, 2008

You can also find useful videos on values and exercises to help establish values on Russ Harris's website here:
www.thehappinesstrap.com

CASAA (The Center on Alcoholism, Substance Abuse abd Additions) at the University of New Mexico provide this useful sheet of value cards, which can be sorted into 'Very Important', 'Important' and 'Not Important' to help establish values:
nhttps://casaa.unm.edu/inst/Personal%20Values%20Card%20Sort.pdf

Emotions
Feldman Barrett, Lisa, *How Emotions are Made: The Secret Life of the Brain*, Pan Macmillan, 2018

Imposter syndrome
Hibberd, Jessamy, Dr., *The Imposter Cure: How to Stop Feeling Like a Fraud and Escape the Mind-Trap of Imposter Syndrome*, Aster, 2019

Change and Goals
Fogg, BJ, *Tiny Habits: The Small Changes that Change Everything*, Virgin Books, 2019

Inner Critic
Gilbert, Paul, *The Compassionate Mind*, Constable, 2010

Acknowledgements
To Kerry, Julia and the Quercus book team. This would never have happened without you. Thank you.

To Stuart, Fraser and Evie. I couldn't have done this without you. Love you.

To my parents. For the space, tea and encouragement. Thank you.

Index

First published in Great Britain in 2020 by

Greenfinch
An imprint of Quercus Editions Ltd
Carmelite House
50 Victoria Embankment
London EC4Y 0DZ

An Hachette UK company

A CIP catalogue record for this book is available from the British Library

HB ISBN 978-1-52941-022-8
E-book ISBN 978-1-52941-023-5

10 9 8 7 6 5 4

Design by Ginny Zeal
Illustrations by Emma Hepburn

Concept of the jam jar model of mental health on p.10 adapted from *How To Talk To Families About Genetics And Psychiatric Illness* by Holly Landrum Peay, Jehannine Claire Austin. Publisher W. W. Norton.

Printed and bound in Croatia by Denona

Papers used by Greenfinch are from well-managed forests and other responsible sources